How to Summit Mount Everest: A Complete Travel and Tourist Guide

Tourist Guide's

Veena Singh Chauhan

Published by Veena Singh Chauhan, 2024.

How to Summit
Mount Everest

A Complete Travel and Tourist Guide

Veena Singh Chauhan

Published by Veena Singh Chauhan, 2024.

How to Summit Mount Everest: A Complete Travel and Tourist Guide.

First edition. February 01, 2024.

Table of Content

Introduction

WELCOME TO "HOW TO Summit Mount Everest: A Complete Travel and Tourist Guide." This book is designed to be your comprehensive companion on the incredible journey of summiting the highest peak in the world. Whether you're an experienced mountaineer or a passionate adventurer looking to fulfill a lifelong dream, this guide will provide you with the knowledge, preparation, and inspiration needed to embark on this extraordinary challenge.

Mount Everest, known as Sagarmatha in Nepal and Chomolungma in Tibet, stands at a staggering 8,848 meters (29,029 feet) above sea level. It has captivated the imagination of explorers and climbers for over a century, symbolizing the ultimate test of human endurance, perseverance, and courage. The allure of Everest lies not only in its height but also in the sheer difficulty and danger associated with reaching its summit.

The History of Mount Everest Exploration

THE HISTORY OF MOUNT Everest exploration is a tale of determination, innovation, and, often, tragedy. Mount Everest, known as Chomolungma ("Goddess Mother of the World") by the Tibetans and Sagarmatha ("Peak of Heaven") by the Nepalese, has been revered by local communities for centuries. However, it wasn't until the mid-19th century that the mountain captured the Western imagination. Through the Great Trigonometrical Survey of India, British surveyors identified Everest as the world's highest peak in 1856, forever etching its name in the annals of exploration.

The first serious attempts to climb Everest began in the early 20th century, with expeditions organized by British mountaineers. George Mallory and Andrew Irvine made a famous attempt in June 8 1924, but their fate remains a mystery, sparking one of the greatest debates in mountaineering history: Did they reach the summit before perishing on the descent?

It wasn't until May 29, 1953, that Sir Edmund Hillary of New Zealand and Tenzing Norgay, a Sherpa of Nepalese Indian, successfully reached the summit, marking a monumental achievement in human history. Their triumph was celebrated worldwide and opened the door for many more climbers to follow in their footsteps. Since then, thousands of climbers from all over the globe have aspired to replicate their success, each bringing their own story to the rich tapestry of Everest lore.

Importance and Allure of Everest

MOUNT EVEREST REPRESENTS more than just a physical challenge; it embodies the spirit of adventure and the human desire to push boundaries. For many, standing on the summit of Everest is a symbol of personal achievement, a testament to their ability to overcome adversity, and a demonstration of their resilience. The mountain's harsh and unpredictable conditions demand a high level of respect and preparation, making every successful ascent a remarkable feat.

Everest's allure also lies in its cultural significance. For the Sherpa people, the mountain is sacred, known as the *"Mother of the World."* Climbing Everest is not just an adventure; it's an opportunity to engage with and respect the rich cultural heritage of the region. The journey to the summit involves more than physical climbing; it's an immersive experience that includes understanding and appreciating the traditions and lifestyles of the local communities.

A Comprehensive Guide to Your Journey

THIS GUIDE AIMS TO provide a detailed roadmap for your journey to the summit of Mount Everest. It covers every aspect of the climb, from initial preparations and training to the final push for the summit and the safe return home. Each chapter is designed to offer practical advice, expert insights, and motivational stories to support you every step of the way.

We will start with an overview of Mount Everest, its geography, and the key landmarks you'll encounter on your climb. Understanding the mountain's terrain and weather conditions is crucial for planning a successful expedition.

Next, we'll delve into the physical and mental preparation required for such a demanding climb. Building the necessary endurance, strength, and mental resilience is essential for tackling the challenges you'll face on the mountain. We'll also discuss health considerations, including altitude sickness and necessary immunizations, to ensure you're physically ready for the ascent.

The gear and equipment chapter will guide you through the essential items you'll need, from clothing and climbing gear to modern technology that can aid in navigation and communication. Choosing the right equipment can make a significant difference in your comfort and safety on the mountain.

Choosing a route and selecting a guide and support team are critical decisions that will greatly influence your experience. We'll explore the main routes to the summit, their pros and cons, and provide tips on selecting a reputable expedition company. Understanding the role of Sherpas and support staff will also be covered, highlighting the importance of their contributions to your success.

The journey to Base Camp and the acclimatization process are next, setting the stage for the climb itself. We'll provide detailed information on travel logistics, trekking to Base Camp, and the importance of gradual ascent to allow your body to adjust to the high altitude.

Once on the mountain, camp life and the climb itself present unique challenges. From managing limited facilities and conserving energy to navigating the treacherous routes from Base Camp to the summit, each stage of the climb requires careful planning and execution. We'll offer a step-by-step guide, including strategies for summit day and tips for maintaining your physical and mental health in the extreme conditions of the Death Zone.

Finally, we'll discuss the descent and post-climb considerations. Safely descending the mountain is as crucial as the ascent, and managing fatigue and resources is key to returning home safely. We'll also cover the recovery process, sharing your experience, and the ethical considerations of climbing Everest.

In addition to the main content, we've included appendices with a sample packing list, emergency contact numbers, and a glossary of climbing terms. These resources will provide quick reference points as you prepare for and undertake your climb.

Inspirational Stories and Quotes

Throughout the guide, you'll find inspirational stories and quotes from climbers who have faced the challenges of Everest and emerged victorious. These narratives serve as a reminder that while the climb is undoubtedly difficult, it is also immensely rewarding. Their experiences can offer motivation and insight as you prepare for your own journey.

Embarking on the journey to summit Mount Everest is not just about reaching the highest point on Earth; it's about discovering the heights of your own potential. This guide is here to support you, providing the tools, knowledge, and encouragement you need to achieve your dream. Welcome to the adventure of a lifetime.

So, if you are an experienced climber with a burning desire to stand atop the world, then turn the page and embark on this extraordinary adventure. With meticulous planning, unwavering dedication, and the wisdom gleaned from this guide, you too may one day find yourself gazing out from the pinnacle of Everest, forever changed by the experience.

Chapter 1:
Understanding the Mount Everest

Geography and Location

MOUNT EVEREST, THE tallest mountain in the world, is part of the Himalaya range in Asia. Its peak, a pyramid of rock and ice, pierces the sky at a staggering 8,848.86 meters (29,032 feet) above sea level. The surrounding terrain is no less formidable. Jagged ridges, colossal glaciers, and deep valleys create a landscape of breathtaking beauty and immense danger. It straddles the border between Nepal to the south and the Tibet Autonomous Region of China to the north. Everest's precise height has been a matter of debate, but it is widely accepted to be 8,848 meters (29,029 feet) above sea level, based on a 1955 Indian survey. More recent measurements, including a 2020 agreement between China and Nepal, confirm this height.

Everest is located in the Mahalangur section of the Himalayas and is part of the Seven Summits, the highest mountains on each of the seven continents. The mountain, known as Sagarmatha in Nepali and Chomolungma in Tibetan, holds great significance in both local cultures. The area surrounding Everest is characterized by its dramatic landscapes, including deep valleys, towering peaks, and an array of glaciers.

Weather and Climate Conditions

THE WEATHER AND CLIMATE conditions on Mount Everest are notoriously harsh and unpredictable, posing significant challenges to climbers. The mountain's climate is influenced by its altitude, resulting in extremely low temperatures, high winds, and a severe lack of oxygen.

Seasons

1. Spring (Pre-Monsoon, April to May): This is the most popular climbing season. The temperatures are relatively milder, and the weather conditions are more stable compared to other times of the year. However, as the season progresses, the risk of avalanches increases due to warming temperatures.

2. Summer (Monsoon, June to September): Heavy monsoon rains make climbing dangerous and difficult. The mountain receives significant precipitation, which can lead to avalanches and landslides. The visibility is poor, and the trails are often muddy and treacherous.

3. Autumn (Post-Monsoon, September to November): This is another favorable season for climbing. The weather is relatively stable, with clear skies and moderate temperatures. The trails are less crowded compared to spring, making it an attractive option for many climbers.

4. Winter (December to February): The extreme cold, high winds, and heavy snowfall make winter climbing highly dangerous. Temperatures can drop below -40°C (-40°F), and the risk of frostbite and hypothermia is very high. Few climbers attempt to summit during this period.

Weather Phenomena

- JET STREAM: THE JET stream, a high-altitude wind current, often passes over Everest, bringing winds of up to 200 mph (320 km/h). These winds can create hazardous conditions for climbers, making it nearly impossible to progress without shelter.

- Sudden Storms: Sudden and severe storms are common on Everest. These can bring heavy snowfall, whiteout conditions, and rapidly falling temperatures, posing serious risks to climbers.

- Temperature Variations: Temperatures on Everest vary significantly between day and night. During the day, temperatures can be slightly above freezing, while at night they can plummet to extreme lows, even during the warmer seasons.

Key Landmarks

UNDERSTANDING THE KEY landmarks on Mount Everest is crucial for any climber. These landmarks not only serve as navigational points but also help climbers plan their acclimatization and rest schedules.

Base Camp

EVEREST BASE CAMP (EBC) is the starting point for climbers attempting to summit Everest. There are two main base camps:

- South Base Camp (Nepal): Located at an altitude of 5,364 meters (17,598 feet), this is the more popular base camp, accessible via a trek through the Khumbu Valley. It serves as the staging area for the South Col route.

- North Base Camp (Tibet): Situated at 5,150 meters (16,900 feet), this base camp is used by climbers taking the North Ridge route. Access requires a drive through the Tibetan Plateau, followed by a shorter trek.

Both base camps provide essential facilities and are the first step in the acclimatization process.

Khumbu Icefall

THE KHUMBU ICEFALL is one of the most dangerous and dramatic features on the South Col route. It is a constantly shifting glacier with deep crevasses and towering ice seracs. Climbers navigate this treacherous section using ladders and ropes. The icefall is typically crossed early in the morning when the ice is more stable due to lower temperatures.

Western Cwm

THE WESTERN CWM (PRONOUNCED "coom") is a broad, flat glacial valley located above the Khumbu Icefall, stretching from Camp I to Camp II. Known as the "Valley of Silence," it is surrounded by towering peaks and offers relatively easy walking terrain. However, it can become extremely hot during the day due to the sun reflecting off the surrounding ice and snow.

Lhotse Face

THE LHOTSE FACE IS a steep, icy wall that climbers must ascend to reach Camp III. It rises approximately 1,125 meters (3,690 feet) and is a formidable challenge due to its angle and the risk of falling ice and rock. Fixed ropes are used to assist climbers in scaling this section.

South Col

THE SOUTH COL IS A high-altitude pass at 7,906 meters (25,938 feet), serving as the final camp (Camp IV) before the summit push on the South Col route. It is a barren, windswept saddle between Everest and Lhotse, often referred to as the "Death Zone" due to the extreme altitude and lack of oxygen. Climbers typically spend as little time as possible here, using it as a staging point for their summit attempt.

Hillary Step

THE HILLARY STEP WAS a near-vertical rock face located just below the summit on the southeast ridge. Named after *Sir Edmund Hillary*, it was one of the last significant obstacles before reaching the top. In recent years, the Hillary Step has been reported to have changed, possibly due to *an earthquake in 2015*, making the final ascent slightly less technical but still challenging.

The Summit

THE SUMMIT OF MOUNT Everest is the ultimate goal, standing at 8,848 meters (29,029 feet). It offers a 360-degree view of the Himalayas and a sense of unparalleled achievement. The conditions at the summit are extreme, with temperatures often dropping to -30°C (-22°F) or lower, and the oxygen level is about one-third of that at sea level. Climbers spend only a short time here, typically around 15-30 minutes, to minimize exposure to the harsh conditions.

Understanding these key landmarks and the associated challenges is essential for planning a successful expedition to Mount Everest. Each section of the climb presents unique difficulties, and thorough preparation is crucial for overcoming them and reaching the summit safely.

Chapter 2:
Preparing for the Climb

Physical and Mental Preparation

CLIMBING MOUNT EVEREST is not just a physical challenge; it requires significant mental fortitude and emotional resilience. The combination of extreme physical exertion, high altitude, and unpredictable weather conditions demands comprehensive preparation. This chapter will guide you through the essential physical and mental training required to maximize your chances of a successful summit.

Training Routines

TO PREPARE FOR EVEREST, a well-rounded training routine is crucial. Your training should focus on building strength, endurance, flexibility, and cardiovascular fitness. Here are some key components to include in your regimen:

1. Cardiovascular Training:

- Running: Incorporate long-distance running to build cardiovascular endurance. Aim for at least three to four runs per week, gradually increasing your distance and intensity for become fit.

- Cycling: Biking is an excellent low-impact way to improve cardiovascular fitness. Use both indoor stationary bikes and outdoor cycling routes.

- Swimming: Swimming provides a full-body workout and improves lung capacity, which is essential for high-altitude climbing.

2. Strength Training:

- Leg Strength: Focus on exercises that build leg strength, such as squats, lunges, and step-ups. Strong legs are crucial for climbing and descending the mountain.

- Core Strength: A strong core helps with balance and stability. Include planks, Russian twists, and leg raises in your routine.

- Upper Body Strength: Climbing often involves pulling yourself up steep sections. Incorporate pull-ups, push-ups, and rows to build upper body strength.

3. Flexibility and Balance:

- Yoga: Practicing yoga enhances flexibility, balance, and mental focus. It also helps prevent injuries.

- Stretching: Regular stretching sessions improve flexibility and reduce muscle stiffness, which is vital during long climbs.

4. Hiking and Climbing:

- Day Hikes: Start with shorter hikes carrying a loaded backpack to simulate the conditions you'll face on Everest. Gradually increase the duration and difficulty of these hikes.

- Technical Climbing: Practice climbing on varied terrains and using different techniques, such as rock climbing and ice climbing. Familiarize yourself with the gear and techniques required for Everest.

Endurance Building

BUILDING ENDURANCE is a critical aspect of preparing for Everest. The climb involves long days of sustained physical activity at high altitudes, where oxygen levels are significantly lower. Here are some strategies to build the necessary endurance:

1. Long Duration Workouts:

- Back-to-Back Training Days: Schedule long hikes or climbs on consecutive days to mimic the endurance demands of a multi-day ascent.

- Extended Sessions: Engage in activities that last several hours, such as marathon training, long-distance cycling, or extended hikes. These sessions help your body adapt to prolonged physical exertion.

2. Altitude Training:

- High-Altitude Hikes: Whenever possible, train at high altitudes to acclimate your body to reduced oxygen levels. This could involve hiking in mountainous regions or using high-altitude training facilities.

- Hypoxic Training: Consider using hypoxic training masks or sleeping in hypoxic tents to simulate high-altitude conditions. This can help your body adapt to lower oxygen levels and improve performance at altitude.

3. Interval Training:

- High-Intensity Interval Training (HIIT): Incorporate HIIT workouts to improve cardiovascular fitness and endurance. These workouts help in involve short bursts of intense exercise followed by periods of rest or lower intensity.

- Fartlek Training: This is a form of interval training where you vary your pace during a run. It improves speed and endurance, making it beneficial for the varied pace of mountaineering.

4. Consistency and Progression:

- Regular Training: Maintain a consistent training schedule, gradually increasing the intensity and duration of your workouts. Consistency is key to building endurance.

- Monitor Progress: Keep track of your training progress, noting improvements in endurance and strength. Adjust your training according plan as needed to ensure continuous progress.

Note: - Rest and Recovery: Remember, your body is a machine, and just like any machine, it needs rest to perform optimally. Schedule regular recovery days to allow your muscles to repair and rebuild. Don't push yourself to the point of injury; a well-rested and healthy climber is a safe climber.

Mental Preparation

MENTAL PREPARATION is as important as physical training when it comes to climbing Everest. The mental challenges include coping with extreme fatigue, staying motivated during long climbs, and managing the psychological effects of high altitude and isolation. Here are some strategies to enhance your mental resilience:

1. Visualization:

- Mental Rehearsal: Visualize each stage of the climb, from the trek to Base Camp to the final push for the summit. This can help you mentally prepare for the challenges and develop a positive mindset.

- Success Imagery: Picture yourself successfully reaching the summit and descending safely. Positive imagery will be boost your confidence and motivation.

2. Mindfulness and Meditation:

- Meditation Practices: Regular meditation can improve focus, reduce stress, and enhance mental clarity. Practice mindfulness meditation to stay present and calm during the climb.

- Breathing Exercises: Deep breathing exercises can help you manage anxiety and improve oxygen intake, which is especially useful at high altitudes.

3. Stress Management:

- Coping Strategies: Develop strategies to manage stress and stay calm under pressure. This could include techniques like progressive muscle relaxation or journaling.

- Support Network: Lean on your support network, including family, friends, and fellow climbers. Sharing your experiences and concerns can alleviate stress and provide emotional support.

4. Adaptability and Problem-Solving:

- Scenario Planning: Anticipate potential challenges and plan how you will address them. This could involve creating contingency plans for adverse weather or equipment failure.

- Decision-Making: Practice making quick, effective decisions in high-pressure situations. Climbing often requires decisive action, and honing this skill can be critical.

5. Setting Goals:

- Short-Term Goals: Break down the climb into manageable sections and set short-term goals for each stage. Achieving these smaller milestones will be boost your motivation and sense of accomplishment.

- Long-Term Vision: Keep your long-term goal—the summit of Everest—in mind. Remind yourself of why you are undertaking this challenge and what it means to you.

Preparing for the climb of Mount Everest is a comprehensive process that involves both physical and mental training. By following a structured training routine, building endurance, and developing mental resilience, you can equip yourself with the skills and mindset necessary to tackle this formidable challenge. With the right preparation, you will be well on your way to standing on the roof of the world.

Health Considerations

HEALTH CONSIDERATIONS are crucial when preparing to climb Mount Everest. Conquering Everest isn't just about physical prowess and mental fortitude; it's about meticulous attention to your health. The extreme altitude and harsh conditions pose significant risks, making it essential to understand and address potential health issues before and during your expedition. This section will cover the primary health concerns: altitude sickness, immunizations, and necessary medications.

Altitude Sickness

ALTITUDE SICKNESS, also known as acute mountain sickness (AMS), is a common and potentially serious condition that affects climbers at high elevations. It occurs when your body struggles to adapt to the lower oxygen levels at high altitudes. Understanding the symptoms, prevention strategies, and treatments for altitude sickness is critical for a safe ascent.

Symptoms of Altitude Sickness:

- Mild Symptoms:
- Headache
- Nausea and vomiting
- Dizziness
- Fatigue
- Shortness of breath
- Insomnia
- Loss of appetite

- Severe Symptoms (which may indicate HACE or HAPE):

- Severe headache unrelieved by medication
- Persistent nausea and vomiting
- Confusion and decreased mental acuity
- Loss of coordination (ataxia)
- Shortness of breath at rest

- Coughing with frothy or pink sputum (indicative of HAPE)

- Hallucinations or irrational behavior

Types of Altitude Sickness:

- Acute Mountain Sickness (AMS): The most common form, with mild to moderate symptoms that can escalate if not addressed.

- High Altitude Cerebral Edema (HACE): A severe form of AMS where the brain swells with fluid, leading to severe headaches, confusion, and loss of coordination.

- High Altitude Pulmonary Edema (HAPE): A buildup of fluid in the lungs, causing extreme shortness of breath, coughing, and fatigue. HAPE can be life-threatening if not treated promptly.

Prevention and Management:

- Gradual Ascent: Ascend slowly to allow your body to acclimate. Follow the "climb high, sleep low" strategy, where you climb to higher altitudes during the day but return to a lower altitude to sleep.

- Acclimatization: Spend several days at intermediate altitudes before moving higher. The typical schedule includes acclimatization days at strategic points during the climb.

- Hydration: Drink plenty of fluids to stay hydrated. Dehydration can exacerbate altitude sickness.

- Avoid Alcohol and Tobacco: These substances can impair acclimatization and exacerbate symptoms.

- Medications: Consider medications such as acetazolamide (Diamox) to help prevent and reduce symptoms of altitude sickness. Consult with a healthcare professional for proper dosage and usage.

- Monitor Symptoms: Regularly check for signs of altitude sickness. Use tools like pulse oximeters to monitor oxygen saturation levels.

- Descent: If severe symptoms occur, descend to a lower altitude immediately. Descent is the most effective treatment for severe altitude sickness.

Immunizations and Medications

PROPER IMMUNIZATIONS and medications are essential for a safe and healthy Everest expedition. Ensure you are up-to-date on routine vaccinations and consider additional vaccines and medications specific to the region and high-altitude environment.

Routine Vaccinations:

- Tetanus, Diphtheria, and Pertussis (Tdap): Ensure you are vaccinated against these common infections.

- Measles, Mumps, and Rubella (MMR): Confirm you have immunity to these viral diseases.

- Polio: Maintain polio immunization, especially if traveling to regions with polio risk.

- Influenza: An annual flu shot can prevent respiratory infections that could complicate your climb.

Additional Vaccinations:

- Hepatitis A and B: Recommended for travel to Nepal and Tibet due to potential exposure through food, water, or medical treatment.

- Typhoid: Especially important if traveling to rural areas where food and water safety may be a concern.

- Rabies: Consider the rabies vaccine if you'll be spending a lot of time outdoors or in remote areas where access to medical care may be limited.

- Meningococcal Vaccine: For protection against meningitis, especially in crowded living conditions at Base Camp.

Travel Medications:

- Acetazolamide (Diamox): As mentioned, this medication can help prevent and reduce the severity of altitude sickness.

- Dexamethasone: A steroid used to treat severe altitude sickness symptoms like HACE. Only use under medical supervision.

- Nifedipine: This medication can help manage HAPE by reducing pulmonary hypertension.

- Antibiotics: Carry a broad-spectrum antibiotic for bacterial infections. Consult your doctor for specific recommendations based on the region and your medical history.

- Anti-diarrheal Medication: Common in travelers to remote regions, medications like loperamide can help manage diarrhea.

- Pain Relievers: Ibuprofen or acetaminophen can alleviate headaches and minor pain associated with climbing and altitude.

- Anti-nausea Medication: Medications like ondansetron can help manage nausea and vomiting caused by altitude sickness or other conditions.

- First Aid Kit: A well-stocked first aid kit should include bandages, antiseptics, blister treatment, and other basic medical supplies.

Preparing Your Medical Kit

In addition to specific medications and immunizations, prepare a comprehensive medical kit tailored for high-altitude climbing. Here are essential items to include:

- Prescription Medications: Ensure you have enough of any personal prescription medications for the duration of the trip.

- Over-the-Counter Medications: Pain relievers, anti-diarrheals, antihistamines, and cold medications.

- Wound Care Supplies: Bandages, gauze, adhesive tape, antiseptic wipes, and antibiotic ointment.

- Blister Treatment: Moleskin, blister pads, and antiseptic ointment.

- Hydration Aids: Oral rehydration salts and electrolyte tablets.

- Oxygen Supply: Portable oxygen cylinders or concentrators, especially for emergency situations at high altitudes.

- Medical Documentation: A copy of your medical history, including allergies, chronic conditions, and medications, as well as emergency contact information.

Preparing for the health challenges of climbing Mount Everest involves thorough planning, including understanding altitude sickness, ensuring proper immunizations, and carrying necessary medications. By taking these precautions, you can mitigate health risks and focus on the exhilarating experience of your climb.

Pre-Climb Health Assessment: Undergo a thorough medical evaluation by a doctor familiar with high-altitude medicine. This assessment will identify any underlying health conditions that could pose a risk on Everest and ensure you're physically fit for the challenge.

Necessary Permits and Paperwork

CLIMBING MOUNT EVEREST involves navigating a series of bureaucratic requirements and securing various permits and paperwork. Properly managing these administrative details is crucial for a smooth and legal expedition. This section will cover the essential permits and insurance requirements.

Climbing Permits

TO CLIMB MOUNT EVEREST, you must obtain specific permits from the respective authorities in Nepal or Tibet, depending on the route you choose. The process can be complex and time-consuming, so it's essential to start early and ensure all documentation is in order.

1. Nepal (South Col Route):
- *Everest Climbing Permit:*
- Issued by: Nepal Ministry of Tourism
- Cost: The permit fee varies depending on the season and the size of the expedition. For spring (the most popular season), the fee is around $11,000 per climber. For autumn, it's around $5,500, and for winter/summer, it's approximately $2,750.
- Application Process: Submit an application to the Ministry of Tourism. You'll need to provide personal details, a climbing plan, and details of your expedition company if you're using one.
- Group Permits: Often, permits are issued to groups rather than individuals, which means you might need to join an expedition team.
- *Sagarmatha National Park Entry Permit:*
- Cost: Approximately $30 per person

- Issued by: Department of National Parks and Wildlife Conservation

- Required for entry into the Sagarmatha National Park, where Everest Base Camp is located.

- *Khumbu Pasang Lhamu Rural Municipality Entrance Permit:*

- Cost: Around $20 per person

- Required for trekkers and climbers entering the Khumbu region.

2. Tibet (North Ridge Route):
- Chinese Visa:

- Issued by: Embassy of the People's Republic of China

- Cost: Varies by nationality

- Application Process: Apply for a tourist visa first, then convert it to a Tibet Travel Permit once in China.

- Tibet Travel Permit:
- Issued by: Tibet Tourism Bureau
- Required for entry into Tibet. Arrange this through a registered travel agency in China.
- Mountaineering License:

- Issued by: Tibet Mountaineering Association
- Cost: Varies by season, but typically around $9,950 to $15,800 per person

- Includes the fee for the climbing permit.

- Alien Travel Permit and Military Permit:

- Required for travel to restricted areas, including Everest Base Camp in Tibet.

- Arranged through your travel agency.

Insurance Requirements

COMPREHENSIVE INSURANCE is essential for an Everest expedition. It provides financial protection against the high costs of medical treatment, evacuation, and other unforeseen expenses. Here's what you need to know about the necessary insurance:

1. Travel Insurance:

- Coverage: Ensure your travel insurance covers trip cancellations, delays, and lost luggage. Given the remote location, flight cancellations due to weather are common, so comprehensive travel coverage is essential.

- Cost: Varies based on the policy and coverage limits. Expect to pay more for policies that cover high-altitude climbing.

2. Medical Insurance:

- Coverage: Your policy must cover medical treatment and hospitalization in Nepal or Tibet. Check for high-altitude coverage, as many standard policies exclude this.

- Pre-existing Conditions: Disclose any pre-existing medical conditions to ensure they are covered.

3. Evacuation Insurance:

- Helicopter Evacuation: Emergency evacuation from Everest can cost tens of thousands of dollars. Ensure your policy covers helicopter evacuation, including from Base Camp and higher altitudes.

- Repatriation: Coverage for repatriation in case of severe injury or death is also crucial.

4. Specialized Climbing Insurance:

- High-Altitude Climbing: Standard insurance policies often exclude high-altitude activities. Purchase specialized climbing insurance that covers altitudes above 6,000 meters.

- Adventure Sports Riders: Some insurers offer add-ons specifically for extreme sports, including mountaineering.

Steps to Secure Permits and Insurance

1. Research and Choose an Expedition Company: - Many climbers opt to join an expedition organized by a reputable company. These companies often handle the permit applications and insurance arrangements, simplifying the process for you.

2. Contact Relevant Authorities: - For independent climbers, contact the Nepal Ministry of Tourism or the Tibet Mountaineering Association directly. Start the application process several months in advance.

3. Gather Required Documentation:
- Prepare necessary documents, including a valid passport, photographs, medical certificates, and proof of insurance.
- If using an expedition company, they will guide you through the required paperwork.

4. Purchase Insurance:
- Compare different insurance providers and policies. Ensure the chosen policy covers all aspects of your climb, including medical treatment, evacuation, and trip cancellations.
- Consider consulting an insurance broker specializing in adventure travel.

5. Budget for Permit Fees and Insurance Costs:

- Factor in the costs of permits and insurance into your overall expedition budget. These can be significant expenses, but they are crucial for a safe and legally compliant climb.

Final Checklist

Before departing for your Everest expedition, ensure you have the following:

- All necessary permits for your chosen route (Nepal or Tibet)
- Comprehensive travel, medical, and evacuation insurance policies
- Copies of all permits and insurance documents
- Emergency contact numbers for your insurance provider
- Confirmation from your expedition company (if applicable) that all arrangements are in place

Securing the necessary permits and insurance is a vital step in preparing for your climb of Mount Everest. By ensuring you have all the required paperwork and coverage, you can focus on the adventure ahead with peace of mind, knowing you are well-prepared for the challenges that await.

Chapter 3:
Essential Gear and Equipment

Clothing and Layering

CLIMBING MOUNT EVEREST requires a careful selection of clothing and gear to protect you from the extreme cold, high winds, and other harsh conditions. Effective layering is critical to regulate body temperature, maintain comfort, and ensure safety. This section will guide you through the necessary clothing and layering strategies, covering base layers, insulation, and outerwear.

Base Layers

BASE LAYERS ARE THE first line of defense against the cold. They are designed to wick moisture away from your skin, keeping you dry and comfortable. Staying dry is essential to prevent hypothermia, especially in the cold and windy conditions on Everest.

1. Materials:

- Merino Wool: Naturally moisture-wicking, odor-resistant, and comfortable. Merino wool is excellent for base layers because it keeps you warm even when wet.

- Synthetic Fabrics: Materials like polyester or nylon blends are also effective at wicking moisture and drying quickly. These fabrics are durable and often less expensive than wool.

2. Garments:

- Base Layer Tops: Long-sleeve tops that fit snugly but comfortably against the skin. Look for features like flatlock seams to prevent chafing.

- Base Layer Bottoms: Full-length bottoms to keep your legs warm. Ensure they are stretchy enough for ease of movement.

3. Weight:

- Lightweight: Best for lower elevations or warmer weather. Lightweight base layers are versatile and can be worn alone in milder conditions.

- Midweight: Suitable for colder conditions and higher elevations. They provide more insulation while still wicking moisture effectively.

- Heavyweight: Used in extremely cold conditions or at high altitudes where extra warmth is crucial. These layers are thicker and provide maximum insulation.

Insulation

INSULATION LAYERS TRAP body heat to keep you warm in the freezing temperatures encountered on Everest. The right insulation is critical to your comfort and safety, particularly at higher altitudes where temperatures can plummet.

1. Types of Insulation:

- Down: Known for its excellent warmth-to-weight ratio. Down insulation is lightweight, compressible, and very warm. However, it loses its insulating properties when wet, so it's best paired with a waterproof outer layer.

- Synthetic: Insulates even when wet and dries quickly. Synthetic insulation is less expensive than down but generally bulkier and heavier.

2. Garments:

- Insulated Jackets: Look for high-fill-power down jackets (700-fill or higher) or high-quality synthetic jackets. Features like adjustable hoods, drawcord hems, and elastic cuffs help seal in warmth.

- Fleece Layers: A fleece jacket or pullover can serve as a versatile mid-layer, providing warmth and breathability.

- Insulated Pants: Down or synthetic insulated pants are essential for higher elevations and cold camps. Ensure they fit comfortably over your base layer bottoms.

3. Layering Strategy:

- Mid-Layer: Typically a fleece or lightweight down/synthetic jacket worn over the base layer. This layer provides insulation while allowing moisture to escape.

- Outer Insulation: A heavier insulated jacket worn during rest breaks, at camp, or in extremely cold conditions. This layer can be added or removed as needed.

Outerwear

OUTERWEAR SERVES AS your protective barrier against the elements, including wind, snow, and rain. It should be durable, waterproof, and breathable to keep you dry and comfortable.

1. Materials:

- Gore-Tex: A popular waterproof and breathable fabric that provides excellent protection against wind and moisture. Gore-Tex and similar materials are highly effective in harsh conditions.

- Other Membranes: Fabrics like eVent and proprietary technologies from various outdoor brands also offer good waterproof and breathable properties.

2. Garments:

- Shell Jackets: A high-quality hardshell jacket is essential for protection against wind and precipitation. Look for features like a helmet-compatible hood, ventilation zippers, and multiple pockets for accessibility.

- Shell Pants: Waterproof and breathable pants that can be worn over insulation layers. Full-length side zippers are useful for easy on/off without removing boots.

- Softshell Jackets/Pants: Useful for lower elevations or milder weather. Softshell garments offer a good balance of water resistance, breathability, and flexibility.

3. Features to Look For:

- Hoods: Adjustable and helmet-compatible hoods provide crucial protection for your head and neck.

- Zippers: Waterproof zippers and storm flaps keep moisture out. Ventilation zippers (pit zips) allow for temperature regulation.

- Seams: Fully taped seams prevent water from seeping through the stitching.

- Fit: Ensure your outerwear fits comfortably over all your layers without restricting movement.

Layering Strategy for Everest

EFFECTIVE LAYERING allows you to adjust your clothing to the changing conditions on Everest. Here is a typical layering strategy:

1. Start with a Base Layer:

- Lightweight or midweight top and bottoms to manage moisture.

2. Add an Insulation Layer:

- Fleece or lightweight down/synthetic jacket for added warmth.

- Insulated pants over base layer bottoms if needed.

3. Apply an Outer Layer:

- Waterproof hardshell jacket and pants for wind and moisture protection.

- Use ventilation zippers to regulate body temperature during physical exertion.

4. Additional Layers as Needed:

- Heavy insulated jacket for extremely cold conditions or high-altitude camps.
- Balaclava, hat, and gloves/mittens for head and hand protection

Accessories

- HEADWEAR: A WARM HAT, balaclava, or neck gaiter to protect your head and face.
- Gloves and Mittens: Layered gloves for dexterity and warmth, with waterproof outer mittens for severe conditions.
- Socks: Moisture-wicking and insulating socks, with liners to prevent blisters.
- Gaiters: To prevent snow and debris from entering your boots.

Packing Smart: Remember, every gram counts on Everest. Choose lightweight, high-performance gear where possible. Pack efficiently, prioritizing warmth and functionality over comfort. Expedition companies often provide a detailed gear list, ensuring you have everything you need for a safe and successful climb. Proper clothing and layering are essential for a successful Everest expedition. By choosing the right materials and garments and understanding how to layer effectively, you can maintain comfort and safety in the extreme conditions you'll face on the mountain.

Climbing Gear

CLIMBING MOUNT EVEREST requires specialized gear that is designed to handle the extreme conditions and technical challenges of high-altitude mountaineering. This section covers essential climbing gear, including ropes, crampons, and ice axes.

#Ropes

ROPES ARE A FUNDAMENTAL piece of climbing gear, providing safety and support in various situations, from ascending steep slopes to crossing crevasses. Choosing the right type of rope and understanding its use is critical for a successful climb.

1. Types of Ropes:

- Dynamic Ropes: Designed to stretch under load, dynamic ropes absorb the energy from a fall, reducing the impact force on the climber and gear. These are primarily used for lead climbing and belaying.

- Static Ropes: These ropes have minimal stretch and are used for fixed lines, rappelling, and hauling gear. They are not suitable for catching falls but are essential for stability and efficiency in specific tasks.

2. Rope Specifications:

- Diameter: Typically ranges from 8.5mm to 11mm. Thicker ropes are more durable but heavier, while thinner ropes are lighter but less durable.

- Length: Standard lengths for dynamic ropes are 60 to 70 meters. Static ropes may vary in length depending on their specific use.

3. Key Considerations:

- Durability: Opt for ropes with a durable sheath to withstand the harsh conditions on Everest.

- Dry Treatment: Ropes with a dry treatment repel moisture, preventing them from becoming heavy and frozen in wet and snowy conditions.

- Certification: Ensure ropes are UIAA (International Climbing and Mountaineering Federation) certified for safety and reliability.

#Crampons

CRAMPONS ARE METAL spikes attached to your boots, providing traction on ice and snow. They are essential for navigating the icy and steep terrain of Mount Everest, including the Khumbu Icefall and the Lhotse Face.

1. Types of Crampons:

- Mountaineering Crampons: Designed for general mountaineering, these crampons typically have 10 to 12 points and are suitable for a variety of terrains.

- Technical Ice Climbing Crampons: These crampons have more aggressive points and are designed for steep ice and mixed climbing. They are often used on the more technical sections of Everest.

2. Attachment Systems:

- Strap-On Crampons: Versatile and can fit most boots, but may be less secure than other types.

- Step-In Crampons: Require boots with a rigid sole and compatible toe and heel welts. They offer a secure fit and are quick to put on and take off.

- Hybrid Crampons: Combine features of strap-on and step-in crampons, suitable for a range of boot types.

3. Key Considerations:

- Fit: Ensure a proper fit with your boots to prevent slippage and ensure maximum effectiveness.

- Durability: Opt for stainless steel or chromoly steel crampons for durability and resistance to rust.

- Anti-Balling Plates: These plates prevent snow from accumulating under the crampons, ensuring consistent traction.

Ice Axes

ICE AXES ARE VERSATILE tools used for climbing, self-arresting in case of a fall, and cutting steps in the ice. The right ice axe is critical for safety and efficiency on Everest's icy and steep sections.

1. Types of Ice Axes:

- Mountaineering Axes: Designed for general mountaineering, these axes are longer and have a straight or slightly curved shaft. They are used for support while walking and for self-arrest.

- Technical Ice Axes (Ice Tools): These axes have a more pronounced curve and a shorter shaft, designed for technical ice climbing and steep terrain.

2. Components:

- Head: The head consists of a pick and an adze. The pick is used for climbing and self-arrest, while the adze is used for cutting steps and clearing snow.

- Shaft: The shaft can be straight or curved. Straight shafts are suitable for general mountaineering, while curved shafts provide better clearance on steep terrain.

- Spike: The spike at the bottom of the shaft is used for stability when the axe is plunged into the snow.

3. Key Considerations:

- Length: The length of the ice axe should match your height and intended use. For general mountaineering, the axe should reach your ankle when held at your side. For technical climbing, shorter axes are preferred.

- Weight: Lighter axes are easier to carry but may be less durable. Balance weight with durability based on your specific needs.

- Leashes: Some climbers use leashes to secure the axe to their wrist, preventing loss during a fall. However, many modern climbers prefer leashless designs for greater freedom of movement.

Additional Climbing Gear

WHILE ROPES, CRAMPONS, and ice axes are essential, other climbing gear is also crucial for a successful Everest expedition. Here's a brief overview of additional necessary equipment:

1. Harness: A comfortable, adjustable harness with gear loops for attaching carabiners and other equipment.

2. Carabiners: Locking and non-locking carabiners for securing ropes, anchors, and gear.

3. Belay Device: A device for controlling the rope during belaying and rappelling.

4. Ascenders: Mechanical devices used for climbing fixed ropes, especially useful in the Khumbu Icefall.

5. Descenders: For controlled descents on fixed ropes, you'll need a descender, also known as a rappel device. This allows you to manage the friction of the rope, ensuring a safe and controlled descent.

6. Helmet: A climbing helmet to protect against falling ice and rocks.

7. Prusik Loops: Used for self-rescue and ascending ropes in emergencies.

8. Snow Pickets and Ice Screws: Anchors for securing ropes in snow and ice.

9. Slings and Runners: Used for extending protection and creating anchors.

Tips for Using Climbing Gear

1. Practice: Familiarize yourself with all your gear and practice using it in a safe environment before your expedition.

2. Maintenance: Regularly inspect your gear for wear and damage. Replace any equipment that shows signs of weakness or wear.

3. Organization: Keep your gear organized and accessible. Use gear loops and carabiners to keep essential items within reach.

4. Adaptability: Be prepared to adapt your gear and techniques to the changing conditions on Everest. Flexibility and experience with your equipment are key to handling the diverse challenges you will face.

SAFETY FIRST: Always ensure your climbing gear is certified and in top condition. Inspect ropes for signs of wear and tear. Learn the proper use of each tool under the guidance of experienced instructors before attempting to use them on Everest.

Climbing Mount Everest requires a comprehensive understanding of essential gear and equipment. By selecting the right ropes, crampons, ice axes, and additional climbing gear, and knowing how to use them effectively, you can significantly enhance your safety and success on the mountain.

Technology and Gadgets

IN ADDITION TO TRADITIONAL climbing gear, modern technology and gadgets play a crucial role in ensuring safety, communication, and navigation on Mount Everest. This section will cover essential technology and gadgets, including GPS devices, satellite phones, and oxygen systems.

GPS Devices

GLOBAL POSITIONING System (GPS) devices are invaluable for navigation and tracking your progress on Everest. They help you pinpoint your location, plan routes, and provide critical data in emergencies.

1. Types of GPS Devices:

- Handheld GPS Units: Rugged, portable devices designed for outdoor use. They offer detailed maps, waypoint marking, and tracking features.

- GPS Watches: Wearable devices that combine the functionality of a GPS unit with the convenience of a wristwatch. They are lighter and more compact but may have limited battery life and smaller screens.

2. Key Features:

- Mapping: Preloaded topographic maps or the ability to upload custom maps. Detailed maps are crucial for navigating complex terrain.

- Waypoint Marking: Ability to mark and save specific locations. This feature helps you track important points such as campsites, crevasses, and route changes.

- Tracking: Real-time tracking of your route, which can be reviewed later to analyze your progress and plan future stages of the climb.

- Battery Life: Long battery life is essential for extended expeditions. Consider devices with replaceable batteries or the ability to recharge via solar panels or power banks.

- Weather Resistance: Waterproof and rugged construction to withstand harsh conditions.

3. Popular Models:

- Garmin GPSMAP Series: Known for their durability, comprehensive mapping features, and long battery life.

- Suunto and Garmin GPS Watches: Offer GPS tracking, altimeter, barometer, and heart rate monitoring in a compact, wearable form.

#Satellite Phones

COMMUNICATION IS VITAL on Everest, both for safety and for staying in touch with your support team. Satellite phones provide reliable communication where regular cell service is unavailable.

1. Types of Satellite Phones:

- Handheld Satellite Phones: Portable devices that provide voice, text, and sometimes limited data services. They work anywhere with a clear view of the sky.

- Satellite Messengers: Devices like the Garmin inReach offer text messaging, SOS capabilities, and basic tracking. They are lighter and more compact than traditional satellite phones but may have limited functionality.

2. Key Features:

- Global Coverage: Ensure the phone supports global coverage, particularly for the regions of Nepal and Tibet.

- Battery Life: Long battery life is crucial for extended use. Carry spare batteries or a solar charger to keep the phone operational.

- Durability: Waterproof and rugged construction to withstand extreme weather conditions.

- SOS Functionality: Emergency SOS feature to alert rescue services in case of an emergency.

3. Popular Models:

- Iridium Extreme 9575: Known for its durability, global coverage, and reliable performance in extreme conditions.

- Garmin inReach Explorer+: Combines GPS navigation with satellite messaging and SOS capabilities, offering a versatile option for climbers.

Oxygen Systems

SUPPLEMENTAL OXYGEN is essential for high-altitude climbing on Everest. It helps prevent altitude sickness, improves performance, and increases safety above 8,000 meters (the "Death Zone").

1. Components of Oxygen Systems:

- Oxygen Cylinders: Portable tanks that store compressed oxygen. Ensure you have enough cylinders to cover the ascent and descent.

- Regulators: Devices that control the flow of oxygen from the cylinder to the mask. Adjustable regulators allow you to set the oxygen flow rate according to your needs.

- Masks: Face masks that deliver oxygen to the climber. Look for masks that fit securely and comfortably, minimizing leakage and ensuring efficient oxygen delivery.

- Carrying Systems: Harnesses or backpacks designed to carry oxygen cylinders comfortably. These systems should distribute weight evenly and allow for easy access to the regulator and mask.

2. Using Oxygen Systems:

- Flow Rate Management: Adjust the flow rate based on your activity level and altitude. Higher altitudes and increased physical exertion require higher flow rates.

- Monitoring Supply: Regularly check your oxygen levels and plan cylinder changes in advance to avoid running out of oxygen.

- Training: Practice using the oxygen system before your expedition to ensure you are familiar with its operation and comfortable wearing the mask.

3. Popular Models:

- Summit Oxygen Systems: Known for their reliability and efficiency, these systems are designed specifically for high-altitude mountaineering.

- TopOut Oxygen Systems: Offer user-friendly features and high performance, trusted by many Everest climbers.

Additional Technology and Gadgets

IN ADDITION TO GPS devices, satellite phones, and oxygen systems, several other gadgets can enhance safety and convenience on Everest:

1. Headlamps: Essential for visibility during early morning starts, night climbs, and in camps. Look for headlamps with long battery life, adjustable brightness, and weather-resistant construction.

2. Two-Way Radios: Useful for communication within your team. Ensure they have a long range and are durable enough for harsh conditions.

3. Solar Chargers and Power Banks: Keep your electronic devices charged. Portable solar panels and high-capacity power banks are invaluable for extended expeditions.

4. Weather Instruments: Portable weather stations or apps that provide real-time weather updates can help you make informed decisions about climbing conditions.

5. Cameras: Capture your journey with a durable and weather-resistant camera. Action cameras like GoPros are popular for their compact size and ability to record high-quality video in extreme conditions.

Tips for Using Technology and Gadgets

1. Familiarize Yourself: Learn how to use all your gadgets before the expedition. Practice with them in conditions similar to what you'll encounter on Everest.

2. Spare Batteries: Carry spare batteries for all electronic devices, as cold temperatures can drain battery life quickly.

3. Protect Your Gear: Use waterproof and shockproof cases to protect your gadgets from harsh weather and rough handling.

4. Backup Systems: Have backup options for critical devices like GPS and communication tools in case of failure.

5. Conserve Power: Turn off devices when not in use and use power-saving modes to extend battery life.

TECHNOLOGY AND GADGETS are indispensable tools for modern Everest expeditions. By choosing the right equipment and knowing how to use it effectively, you can enhance your safety, communication, and overall success on the mountain.

Chapter 4:
Choosing a Route

MOUNT EVEREST OFFERS climbers two main routes to the summit: the South Col route from Nepal and the North Ridge route from Tibet. Each route presents its own set of challenges, advantages, and unique experiences. Understanding the key features of these routes will help you make an informed decision about which path to take on your journey to the top of the world.

Overview of Main Routes

#South Col Route (Nepal)

THE SOUTH COL ROUTE is the most popular and historically significant route to the summit of Everest. It was first successfully climbed by Sir Edmund Hillary and Tenzing Norgay in 1953, marking the first confirmed ascent of the mountain. This route begins in Nepal and takes climbers through a series of iconic and challenging landmarks.

1. Starting Point:

- The journey begins in the town of Lukla, where climbers typically fly in from Kathmandu. From Lukla, climbers trek through the Khumbu Valley to reach Everest Base Camp (EBC) at 5,364 meters (17,598 feet).

2. Key Landmarks:

- Khumbu Icefall: One of the most dangerous sections of the climb, the Khumbu Icefall is a moving glacier filled with crevasses and towering ice seracs. Climbers navigate this section using ladders and ropes.

- Western Cwm: A flat, glacial valley that provides a relative respite from the technical challenges of the Icefall. The Cwm leads to Camp II at 6,400 meters (21,000 feet).

- Lhotse Face: A steep, icy slope that climbers must ascend to reach Camp III at 7,200 meters (23,600 feet). Fixed ropes are used for safety.

- South Col: A high-altitude pass and the location of Camp IV at 7,950 meters (26,085 feet). The South Col serves as the launching point for the final push to the summit.

- The Balcony: A small platform at 8,400 meters (27,559 feet) where climbers can rest and check their oxygen supplies.

- Hillary Step: A near-vertical rock face at 8,760 meters (28,740 feet). Named after Sir Edmund Hillary, this section was once a major obstacle but has become more accessible due to changing conditions.

3. Summit Day:

- From the South Col, climbers make their final ascent to the summit at 8,848 meters (29,029 feet). The climb is physically demanding and requires careful pacing, use of supplemental oxygen, and attention to weather conditions.

#North Ridge Route (Tibet)

THE NORTH RIDGE ROUTE is the second most popular route to the summit and offers a different set of challenges compared to the South Col route. This route was first successfully climbed by a Chinese team in 1960. It begins in Tibet and provides a more remote and less crowded experience.

1. Starting Point:

- The journey begins in Lhasa, Tibet, where climbers acclimate before traveling to Everest Base Camp (North) at 5,150 meters (16,896 feet) near the Rongbuk Monastery.

2. Key Landmarks:

- Rongbuk Glacier: Climbers trek across the glacier to reach the Advanced Base Camp (ABC) at 6,400 meters (21,000 feet). ABC serves as a crucial acclimatization point.

- North Col: Climbers ascend the North Col to reach Camp II at approximately 7,000 meters (22,966 feet). This section involves climbing a steep snow slope using fixed ropes.

- North Ridge: The route continues along the North Ridge to reach Camp III at 7,500 meters (24,606 feet). The ridge offers stunning views but is exposed to strong winds.

- Yellow Band: A distinctive rock formation that climbers must traverse to continue their ascent.

- First and Second Steps: Two technical rock sections at 8,500 meters (27,887 feet) and 8,610 meters (28,250 feet), respectively. These steps require careful climbing and are equipped with fixed ladders and ropes.

3. Summit Day:

- From Camp IV at 8,230 meters (27,000 feet), climbers make their final ascent to the summit. The climb includes crossing the Third Step, another rock formation, before reaching the summit pyramid.

Pros and Cons of Each Route

#South Col Route (Nepal)

PROS:
- Historical Significance: Following in the footsteps of the first successful climbers.
- Infrastructure: Better infrastructure and support services in the Khumbu region, including well-established trekking paths, lodges, and medical facilities.
- Community and Culture: Rich cultural experiences in Nepal, with opportunities to interact with the Sherpa community and visit monasteries.
- Higher Success Rate: Statistically, the South Col route has a higher summit success rate, offering a potentially better chance of reaching the top.
  Cons:
- Crowds: The popularity of this route means it can be crowded, especially during peak climbing seasons.
- Khumbu Icefall: The Icefall is one of the most dangerous sections of the climb, with risks of avalanches and ice collapses.

- Exposed to Wind: While not as severe as the North Col, the south face of Everest can experience strong winds, adding a further challenge to the climb.

North Ridge Route (Tibet)

PROS:

- Fewer Crowds: Less crowded than the South Col route, offering a more solitary and remote climbing experience.

- Gradual Ascent: The approach to Advanced Base Camp (ABC) allows for a more gradual acclimatization process.

- Spectacular Views: The North Ridge route offers unparalleled panoramic vistas of the surrounding Himalayas, a unique perspective not available on the South Col route.

- Pure Mountaineering: The steeper terrain and less developed infrastructure present a more technical and challenging climb, appealing to experienced mountaineers seeking a true test of their skills.

Cons:

- Political Restrictions: Access to Tibet can be subject to political restrictions and visa requirements imposed by the Chinese government.

- Technical Challenges: The First and Second Steps are technically demanding and require skillful climbing.

- Weather Exposure: The North Ridge is more exposed to harsh winds and extreme weather conditions.

- Steeper Ascend: The North Col route's steeper profile demands greater physical strength and endurance, making it a more formidable physical challenge.

- Lower Success Rate: Statistically, the North Col route boasts a lower summit success rate, and climbers need to be comfortable with a potentially higher risk factor.

Deciding the Best Route for You

CHOOSING THE BEST ROUTE to summit Everest depends on various factors, including your climbing experience, physical fitness, preference for cultural experiences, and risk tolerance. Consider the following points when making your decision:

1. Experience Level: Less experienced climbers might prefer the South Col route due to its better infrastructure and support. More experienced climbers looking for a technical challenge may opt for the North Ridge route.

2. Crowds: If you prefer a less crowded and more remote experience, the North Ridge route may be more appealing.

3. Cultural Preferences: The South Col route offers rich cultural interactions with the Sherpa community and opportunities to explore the Khumbu region.

4. Technical Skills: Evaluate your technical climbing skills and comfort level with sections like the Khumbu Icefall (South Col) and the First and Second Steps (North Ridge).

5. Weather and Conditions: Stay informed about current weather conditions and route-specific hazards. Consult with expedition leaders and guides to understand the best timing and conditions for your climb.

By thoroughly understanding the South Col and North Ridge routes, you can make an informed choice that aligns with your skills, preferences, and goals for your Everest expedition.

Consulting the Experts: Discuss your options with experienced climbers and your chosen expedition company. Their insights and knowledge of your capabilities will be invaluable in guiding you towards the route that best aligns with your goals and skillset. Remember, there's no shame in choosing the South Col route. Reaching the summit of Everest, regardless of the path, is a monumental achievement.

Chapter 5:
Selecting a Guide and Support Team

Importance of a Guide

CLIMBING MOUNT EVEREST is an extraordinary challenge that requires not only physical endurance and mental resilience but also extensive knowledge of high-altitude mountaineering. Having an experienced guide is crucial for several reasons:

1. Safety: Guides are trained to handle the numerous hazards associated with high-altitude climbing, including crevasses, avalanches, and extreme weather conditions. They are equipped to make critical decisions that can prevent accidents and ensure climbers' safety.

2. Experience and Knowledge: Guides bring invaluable experience, having typically climbed Everest and other high-altitude peaks multiple times. Their knowledge of the route, terrain, and climbing techniques is essential for a successful ascent.

3. Logistical Support: Managing the logistics of an Everest expedition is complex. Guides coordinate the transportation, permits, supplies, and camp setups, allowing climbers to focus on the climb itself.

4. Emergency Response: In the event of an emergency, such as altitude sickness or injury, guides are trained to provide first aid, manage evacuations, and make life-saving decisions.

5. Motivation and Morale: The mental challenges of climbing Everest are significant. Guides offer encouragement, support, and motivation, helping climbers to push through difficult moments and maintain their morale.

How to Choose a Reputable Expedition Company

SELECTING THE RIGHT expedition company is one of the most important decisions you'll make when planning your Everest climb. Here are key factors to consider:

1. Company Reputation:

- Research: Look for companies with a long history of successful Everest expeditions. Read reviews and testimonials from past clients to gauge their reputation.

- Certifications and Memberships: Check if the company is certified by reputable mountaineering organizations such as the International Federation of Mountain Guides Associations (IFMGA) or the American Mountain Guides Association (AMGA).

2. Guides' Experience:

- Credentials: Ensure the guides are certified and have extensive high-altitude climbing experience, particularly on Everest.

- Success Rates: Inquire about the company's summit success rates and safety records.

3. Support Services:

- Logistics: A good expedition company will handle all logistics, including transportation, accommodation, permits, and supplies.

- Medical Support: Ensure the company provides medical support, including oxygen systems, first aid kits, and access to medical professionals if needed.

4. Group Size and Guide-to-Climber Ratio:

- Group Size: Smaller groups often receive more personalized attention and support. Larger groups may offer more social interaction but can be less flexible.

- Guide-to-Climber Ratio: A low guide-to-climber ratio (e.g., 1:3 or 1:4) ensures more individualized attention and better safety management.

5. Cost:

- Transparency: The company should provide a clear breakdown of costs, including what is and isn't included in the price.

- Value: While cost is a consideration, the cheapest option may not provide the best support or safety. Balance cost with the quality of services offered.

6. Ethical Practices:

- Treatment of Sherpas: Ensure the company treats its Sherpa staff fairly, providing them with proper wages, insurance, and equipment.

- Environmental Responsibility: Look for companies that follow environmentally responsible practices, such as minimizing waste and adhering to Leave No Trace principles.

Choosing Your Guide: Look for a certified guide with extensive experience on Everest, particularly on the route you've chosen. Reputation matters – research the guide's background, safety record, and climber testimonials. The ideal guide fosters trust and open communication, making you feel comfortable and confident in their leadership.

Understanding the Roles of Sherpas and Support Staff

SHERPAS AND SUPPORT staff play vital roles in Everest expeditions, providing essential assistance and contributing significantly to the success and safety of climbers. Understanding their roles and the value they bring is crucial.

1. Sherpas:

- High-Altitude Porters: Sherpas are often responsible for carrying heavy loads of equipment and supplies between camps. Their strength and acclimatization to high altitudes are invaluable.

- Route Setting: Experienced Sherpas set up fixed ropes and ladders, particularly in hazardous sections like the Khumbu Icefall, ensuring safe passage for climbers.

- Guiding and Support: Many Sherpas serve as assistant guides, providing guidance, support, and encouragement to climbers. They often accompany climbers on summit day, offering critical assistance.

- Cultural Ambassadors: Sherpas share their rich cultural heritage and knowledge of the mountains, enhancing the overall experience of the expedition.

2. Support Staff:

- Base Camp Managers: These staff members oversee the logistics and operations at Base Camp, coordinating supplies, communication, and support services.

- Cooks and Kitchen Staff: Providing nutritious and high-energy meals, kitchen staff play a crucial role in maintaining climbers' health and energy levels throughout the expedition.

- Yak Drivers and Porters: Responsible for transporting equipment and supplies from lower elevations to Base Camp, these staff members are essential for the smooth operation of the expedition.

3. Tips for Working with Sherpas and Support Staff:

- Respect and Appreciation: Remember, Sherpas are your partners, not your servants. Show respect and appreciation for the hard work and dedication of Sherpas and support staff. Their contributions are critical to the success of your climb.

- Communication: Maintain open and respectful communication with the team. Understand their roles and follow their guidance, particularly in challenging situations.

- Cultural Sensitivity: Learn about and respect the cultural traditions and practices of the Sherpa community. Building a positive relationship with the team enhances the overall experience.

Selecting a guide and support team is one of the most critical aspects of preparing for an Everest expedition. A reputable expedition company, experienced guides, and dedicated Sherpas and support staff provide the foundation for a safe, successful, and enriching journey to the summit of Mount Everest.

Chapter 6:
The Journey to Base Camp

Travel Logistics

BEFORE YOU CAN BEGIN your ascent of Mount Everest, you need to reach Everest Base Camp, the starting point for your climb. This journey involves several logistical steps, including international flights, in-country travel, and a trek to Base Camp. This chapter will guide you through the travel logistics to ensure you arrive at Base Camp prepared and ready for the climb ahead.

#Flights to Nepal/Tibet

#Nepal Route (South Col)

1. INTERNATIONAL FLIGHT to Kathmandu:
  - Booking: Book your international flight to Tribhuvan International Airport in Kathmandu, Nepal. Ensure you arrive a few days before your scheduled trek to allow for any travel delays and to acclimate to the new environment.
  - Visas: Obtain a tourist visa for Nepal. You can get a visa on arrival at the airport or apply online before your trip. Make sure your passport is valid for at least six months beyond your intended stay.
  2. Domestic Flight to Lukla:
  - Booking: Book a domestic flight from Kathmandu to Tenzing-Hillary Airport in Lukla. This small airport is the gateway to

the Everest region. Flights are often scheduled early in the morning to avoid afternoon weather disruptions.

- Flight Experience: The flight to Lukla is an adventure in itself, offering stunning views of the Himalayas. However, it is also known for being one of the most challenging flights due to the short runway and mountainous terrain.

- Contingency Plans: Be prepared for potential delays or cancellations due to weather conditions. Consider scheduling buffer days in your itinerary to accommodate these uncertainties.

#Tibet Route (North Ridge

1. INTERNATIONAL FLIGHT to Lhasa:

- Booking: Book an international flight to Lhasa Gonggar Airport in Tibet. Most climbers fly to Lhasa from Kathmandu, Nepal, or from major Chinese cities like Beijing or Chengdu.

- Visas and Permits: Obtain a Chinese visa and a special Tibet Travel Permit. These permits are typically arranged by your expedition company. Ensure all documents are in order before your departure.

2. Travel to Base Camp:

- Overland Journey: From Lhasa, travel overland to Everest Base Camp (North). This journey involves a drive of several days, passing through high-altitude Tibetan landscapes and stopping at towns like Shigatse and Tingri for acclimatization.

- Altitude Consideration: The overland journey allows for gradual acclimatization to high altitudes, reducing the risk of altitude sickness. Your expedition company will manage the logistics and ensure you acclimate properly.

Trekking to Base Camp

REACHING EVEREST BASE Camp requires a multi-day trek through some of the most breathtaking landscapes on earth. The trek not only prepares you physically for the climb but also provides an opportunity to acclimate to the altitude and immerse yourself in the local culture.

#Nepal Route (South Col)

1. TREK FROM LUKLA to Everest Base Camp:
   - Day 1: Lukla to Phakding: After arriving in Lukla, the trek begins with a relatively easy hike to Phakding (2,610 meters/8,562 feet). This initial trek helps you get used to walking at altitude.
   - Day 2: Phakding to Namche Bazaar: The trek continues to Namche Bazaar (3,440 meters/11,286 feet), the main trading hub of the Khumbu region. This segment includes crossing suspension bridges and ascending through pine forests.
   - Acclimatization Days: Spend a couple of days in Namche Bazaar to acclimate. Take short hikes to higher altitudes, such as the Everest View Hotel or Khumjung village, before returning to Namche to sleep.
   - Namche Bazaar to Tengboche: The trek from Namche to Tengboche (3,860 meters/12,664 feet) includes stunning views of Everest, Ama Dablam, and other peaks. Visit the famous Tengboche Monastery for a spiritual boost.
   - Tengboche to Dingboche: Continue to Dingboche (4,410 meters/14,468 feet), where you will spend another acclimatization day. The landscape becomes more barren, and you will notice the thinning air.
   - Dingboche to Lobuche: The trek from Dingboche to Lobuche (4,940 meters/16,207 feet) passes through the memorial area of Chukpo Lari, dedicated to climbers who lost their lives on Everest.

- Lobuche to Gorak Shep and Everest Base Camp: The final leg of the trek takes you to Gorak Shep (5,170 meters/16,961 feet) and then on to Everest Base Camp (5,364 meters/17,598 feet). Celebrate your arrival at Base Camp, where you will prepare for the climb ahead.

2. Key Considerations:

- Acclimatization: Take your time to acclimate properly. Listen to your body and follow the acclimatization schedule provided by your expedition company.

- Hydration and Nutrition: Stay hydrated and eat nutritious meals to maintain your energy levels. High-altitude trekking requires more calories, so focus on a balanced diet rich in carbohydrates and proteins.

- Gear and Clothing: Wear appropriate gear and clothing for the varying weather conditions. Layering is key to staying comfortable and warm.

#Tibet Route (North Ridge)

1. TRAVEL FROM LHASA to Everest Base Camp:

- Day 1-2: Lhasa to Shigatse: Drive from Lhasa to Shigatse (3,800 meters/12,467 feet), the second-largest city in Tibet. Visit the Tashilhunpo Monastery and explore the local culture.

- Day 3-4: Shigatse to Tingri: Continue the journey to Tingri (4,300 meters/14,108 feet), a small town that serves as an acclimatization stop. Spend an extra day here to acclimate.

- Tingri to Everest Base Camp (North): The final leg takes you to Everest Base Camp (North) at 5,150 meters (16,896 feet). The drive offers panoramic views of Everest and the surrounding peaks.

2. Key Considerations:

- Acclimatization: The overland journey provides gradual acclimatization. Follow your expedition leader's advice to minimize the risk of altitude sickness.

- Hydration and Nutrition: Stay hydrated and eat well to maintain energy levels during the drive and upon arrival at Base Camp.

- Gear and Clothing: Prepare for the cold and windy conditions of the Tibetan plateau. Layering and proper gear are essential for comfort.

Additional Tips for the Journey to Base Camp

1. PERMITS AND DOCUMENTATION: Ensure you have all necessary permits and documentation before starting your journey. Your expedition company will typically assist with this process.

2. Health Precautions: Take any required vaccinations and carry a basic medical kit. Consult your doctor about medications for altitude sickness and other potential health issues.

3. Travel Insurance: Obtain comprehensive travel insurance that covers high-altitude trekking and mountaineering. Ensure it includes emergency evacuation coverage.

4. Packing: Pack essential gear and clothing, but keep your load manageable. Your expedition company will provide a detailed packing list.

5. Mental Preparation: The journey to Base Camp is both physically and mentally demanding. Stay positive, take in the stunning scenery, and enjoy the unique cultural experiences along the way.

Reaching Everest Base Camp is an achievement in itself and sets the stage for the challenging climb to come. Proper planning, acclimatization, and logistical preparation are key to ensuring a successful and enjoyable journey to Base Camp.

Acclimatization Process

ACCLIMATIZATION IS a critical process in preparing your body to cope with the decreased oxygen levels at high altitudes. Proper acclimatization can help prevent altitude sickness and improve your chances of a successful ascent. This section outlines the importance of gradual ascent and provides a suggested acclimatization schedule to follow during your trek to Everest Base Camp.

Importance of Gradual Ascent

1. UNDERSTANDING ALTITUDE Sickness:

- Types of Altitude Sickness: There are three main types of altitude sickness: Acute Mountain Sickness (AMS), High Altitude Pulmonary Edema (HAPE), and High Altitude Cerebral Edema (HACE). AMS is the most common and can progress to the more severe HAPE and HACE if not addressed.

- Symptoms: Common symptoms of AMS include headache, nausea, dizziness, fatigue, and difficulty sleeping. Severe symptoms, such as persistent cough, shortness of breath, and confusion, may indicate HAPE or HACE and require immediate medical attention.

2. Physiological Changes:

- Oxygen Levels: As altitude increases, the air becomes thinner, and the oxygen levels decrease. Your body needs time to adapt to these changes by producing more red blood cells and enhancing oxygen delivery to tissues.

- Hydration: Staying well-hydrated is crucial as high altitudes can lead to increased fluid loss through respiration and perspiration.

3. Key Principles of Acclimatization:

- Climb High, Sleep Low: This principle involves ascending to a higher altitude during the day and descending to a lower altitude to sleep, helping your body adjust gradually.

- Gradual Ascent: Limit daily altitude gains to 300-500 meters (1,000-1,500 feet) above 3,000 meters (10,000 feet). Incorporate rest days to allow your body to acclimate.

- Listening to Your Body: Pay attention to your body's signals. If you experience symptoms of altitude sickness, do not ascend further until you feel better. If symptoms persist or worsen, descend immediately.

#Suggested Acclimatization Schedule

FOLLOWING A STRUCTURED acclimatization schedule can significantly enhance your ability to adjust to high altitudes. Here's a suggested schedule for the trek to Everest Base Camp (South Col route):

1. Day 1: Arrive in Lukla (2,860 meters / 9,383 feet) and Trek to Phakding (2,610 meters / 8,562 feet)

- Duration: 3-4 hours

- Acclimatization: Take it easy on this initial trek. Focus on staying hydrated and adjusting to the altitude.

2. Day 2: Phakding to Namche Bazaar (3,440 meters / 11,286 feet)

- Duration: 5-6 hours

- Acclimatization: Gradual ascent with several suspension bridge crossings. Take it slow and enjoy the stunning views.

3. Day 3: Acclimatization Day in Namche Bazaar

- Activity: Short hikes to higher altitudes (e.g., Everest View Hotel at 3,880 meters / 12,729 feet) and return to Namche to sleep.

- Acclimatization: Helps your body adjust to the altitude. Explore Namche Bazaar and visit local attractions.

4. Day 4: Namche Bazaar to Tengboche (3,860 meters / 12,664 feet)

- Duration: 5-6 hours

- Acclimatization: Gradual climb with an ascent through rhododendron forests. Visit Tengboche Monastery.

5. Day 5: Tengboche to Dingboche (4,410 meters / 14,468 feet)

- Duration: 5-6 hours

- Acclimatization: Continue the gradual ascent. The landscape becomes more barren and rugged.

6. Day 6: Acclimatization Day in Dingboche

- Activity: Hike to Nagarjun Hill (5,100 meters / 16,732 feet) or Chukhung Valley and return to Dingboche.

- Acclimatization: Critical for adjusting to higher altitudes. Rest and hydrate well.

7. Day 7: Dingboche to Lobuche (4,940 meters / 16,207 feet)

- Duration: 5-6 hours

- Acclimatization: The trail becomes steeper and more challenging. Take your time and enjoy the views.

8. Day 8: Lobuche to Gorak Shep (5,170 meters / 16,961 feet) and Everest Base Camp (5,364 meters / 17,598 feet)

- Duration: 7-8 hours (round trip)

- Acclimatization: The final push to Base Camp. Rest frequently and monitor your body's response to the altitude.

9. Day 9: Hike to Kala Patthar (5,545 meters / 18,192 feet) and Return to Pheriche (4,371 meters / 14,340 feet)

- Duration: 7-8 hours

- Acclimatization: Ascend to Kala Patthar for stunning views of Everest. Descend to Pheriche for better sleep and recovery.

10. Day 10: Pheriche to Namche Bazaar

- Duration: 6-7 hours

- Acclimatization: Descending to lower altitudes will help your body recover.

11. Day 11: Namche Bazaar to Lukla

- Duration: 6-7 hours

- Acclimatization: Completing the trek with a descent to Lukla.

Additional Acclimatization Tips

1. STAY HYDRATED: DRINK plenty of fluids, such as water, tea, and soups. Avoid alcohol and caffeine, as they can lead to dehydration.

2. Eat Nutritious Foods: Focus on a balanced diet with plenty of carbohydrates to provide energy. Small, frequent meals are easier to digest at high altitudes.

3. Sleep Well: Ensure you get adequate rest. Sleeping at high altitudes can be challenging, so use earplugs and an eye mask if necessary.

4. Monitor Your Health: Regularly check your oxygen saturation levels using a pulse oximeter if available. Report any symptoms of altitude sickness to your guide immediately.

5. Slow and Steady: Pace yourself and avoid overexertion. Trekking at high altitudes is not a race, and a steady, deliberate pace is key to acclimatization.

6. Mental Preparation: Stay positive and mentally prepared for the challenges of high-altitude trekking. Take in the stunning scenery and enjoy the journey.

Proper acclimatization is essential for a successful and safe trek to Everest Base Camp. By following a gradual ascent and paying attention to your body's needs, you can minimize the risks of altitude sickness and fully enjoy this incredible journey.

Chapter 7:
Camp Life on Everest

Limited Facilities and the Importance of Proper Camp Hygiene

LIVING AT HIGH ALTITUDES on Mount Everest presents unique challenges, particularly in terms of facilities and hygiene. Proper camp hygiene is crucial to maintaining health and preventing illness, which can be detrimental to your climb.

1. Sanitation Facilities:

- Living Quarters: You'll reside in a pre-fabricated expedition tent, often shared with a few teammates. Space is limited, so pack light and be prepared for close quarters. Sleeping bags rated for extreme cold temperatures are essential.

- Toilets: Facilities at Base Camp and higher camps are rudimentary. At Base Camp, you'll typically find makeshift toilets, often tents with barrels or pits. Higher up, climbers use portable toilet bags.

- Waste Management: Proper waste disposal is essential. Many expedition companies follow strict guidelines to carry all waste back to Base Camp for disposal. Some even have eco-friendly waste management systems.

2. Water Supply:

- Water Sources: Water is usually sourced from glacial streams, which require purification. Boiling water, using water purification tablets, or portable water filters are common methods.

- Hydration: Staying hydrated is vital. Dehydration can exacerbate the effects of altitude sickness and reduce physical performance. Drink at least 3-4 liters of water daily.

3. Food Preparation and Storage:

- Meal Preparation: Meals are often prepared by cooks at Base Camp. Above Base Camp, meals are simpler and usually consist of dehydrated or pre-packaged foods.

- Hygiene Practices: Ensure that all food preparation surfaces and utensils are clean. Use hand sanitizer before eating or handling food.

4. Personal Hygiene:

- Hand Washing: Frequent hand washing with soap and water or using hand sanitizer is crucial. This reduces the risk of gastrointestinal illnesses.

- Bathing: Bathing options are limited. At Base Camp, you might have access to solar showers or warm water buckets. Higher camps do not have such facilities, so wet wipes are often used.

5. Cleanliness of Camps:

- Camp Setup: Keep your tent clean and organized. Store gear and clothing in waterproof bags to protect them from moisture and dirt.

- Environmental Responsibility: Follow Leave No Trace principles. Pack out all waste, including trash and used batteries. Respect the pristine environment.

Managing Sleep, Eating, and Conserving Energy at High Altitude

SLEEPING SOUNDLY ABOVE 5,000 meters can be a challenge. Managing your basic needs at high altitudes is crucial to maintaining your health and energy levels for the climb ahead.

1. Sleep:

- Challenges of Sleeping at Altitude: Sleeping at high altitudes can be difficult due to reduced oxygen levels, cold temperatures, and noisy environments. Insomnia and frequent waking are common.

- Improving Sleep Quality:

- Warmth: Use a high-quality sleeping bag rated for extreme cold. Sleeping in layers and using a sleeping pad for insulation from the ground can help.

- Earplugs and Eye Masks: These can block out noise and light, improving sleep quality.

- Breathing Techniques: Practice deep breathing or use techniques like the "Buteyko Method" to improve oxygen intake.

- Regular Sleep Schedule: Try to maintain a regular sleep schedule. Going to bed and waking up at the same time each day helps regulate your body clock.

2. Eating:

- Nutritional Needs at High Altitude: Your body requires more calories at high altitudes due to increased energy expenditure and the cold environment.

- Types of Food:

- High-Calorie Foods: Focus on high-calorie, nutrient-dense foods like nuts, dried fruits, energy bars, and chocolates.

- Carbohydrates: Carbohydrates are the body's preferred energy source at high altitudes. Include pasta, rice, bread, and potatoes in your diet.

- Hydration: Soups and hot drinks not only provide fluids but also warmth. Avoid alcohol and caffeine as they can lead to dehydration.

- Appetite Changes: Altitude can suppress appetite, so eat small, frequent meals rather than large ones. Listen to your body and eat whenever you feel hungry.

3. Conserving Energy:

- Pacing Yourself:

- Slow and Steady: Move at a steady, manageable pace. Overexertion can lead to fatigue and increase the risk of altitude sickness.

- Rest Breaks: Take regular short breaks to rest and hydrate, but avoid long rests that can cause your body to cool down too much.

- Efficient Movement:

- Minimal Effort: Use efficient techniques for climbing and walking to conserve energy. Practice proper foot placement and use of climbing gear to reduce exertion.

- Light Load: Keep your backpack light. Only carry essential items during acclimatization hikes and summit pushes. Leave non-essentials at lower camps.

- Mental Conservation:

- Positive Mindset: Maintain a positive attitude. Mental fatigue can be as draining as physical fatigue.

- Relaxation Techniques: Practice relaxation techniques like deep breathing, meditation, or visualization to reduce stress and conserve mental energy.

4. Clothing and Gear:

- Layering: Use a layered clothing system to regulate body temperature efficiently. Remove or add layers based on activity level and weather conditions.

- Proper Gear: Ensure all your gear is appropriate for high-altitude conditions. This includes insulated clothing, gloves, hats, and proper footwear.

- Protective Equipment: Use sunglasses and sunscreen to protect against the intense UV radiation at high altitudes.

Conserving Energy: Base camp life may seem relaxed, but it's vital to conserve energy for the demanding climb ahead. Avoid strenuous activity and prioritize rest. Delegate tasks whenever possible and embrace a slower pace of life.

Mental Toughness: Life at EBC can be monotonous and mentally challenging. Prepare yourself for long periods of inactivity punctuated by bursts of activity during acclimatization rotations. Find healthy ways to occupy your time – read, write, meditate, or simply enjoy the awe-inspiring scenery.

Living at high altitudes requires careful management of your body's needs and adapting to the limited facilities available. Prioritizing hygiene, sleep, nutrition, and energy conservation will help you stay healthy and strong as you prepare for the challenging climb to the summit of Mount Everest.

Chapter 8:
The Climb

Step-by-Step Guide from Base Camp to Summit

EVEREST BASE CAMP (EBC) is behind you, and the air thins as you embark on the most challenging leg of your journey – the summit push. Climbing Mount Everest is a monumental task that requires careful planning and execution. This step-by-step guide will take you through the key stages of the climb from Base Camp to the summit. Each stage presents unique challenges and requires specific strategies to ensure a successful ascent.

Remember: Safety is paramount. This guide is a general overview, and your expedition leader will make final decisions based on weather conditions and climber fitness. Be prepared to adapt and prioritize your safety throughout the climb.

Base Camp to Camp I

ELEVATION:
- Base Camp: 5,364 meters (17,598 feet)
- Camp I: 6,065 meters (19,900 feet)
Distance: Approximately 9 km (5.6 miles)
Terrain: Khumbu Icefall Collapse Zone
Key Challenges:
- Navigating through the Khumbu Icefall, a constantly shifting glacier.

- Crossing crevasses using ladders.
- Dealing with ice blocks and potential avalanches.
Guide:

1. Early Start: Begin the climb early in the morning to avoid the heat and instability of the icefall in the afternoon.

2. Rope Teams: Move in rope teams for safety. Experienced Sherpas will lead and secure the route.

3. Crevasse Crossings: Carefully cross crevasses using ladders. Use a safety line at all times.

4. Pace and Hydration: Maintain a steady pace and stay hydrated. Take short breaks as needed.

Camp I to Camp II

ELEVATION:
- Camp I: 6,065 meters (19,900 feet)
- Camp II: 6,400 meters (21,000 feet)
Distance: Approximately 3 km (1.9 miles)
Terrain: Western Cwm
Key Challenges:
- Traversing the flat, but deceptively challenging Western Cwm.
- Managing the heat, as the Cwm can act like a solar oven.
Guide:

1. Moderate Ascent: The climb is less steep but requires stamina. The main challenge is the heat and the reflective snow.

2. Stay Hydrated: Drink plenty of water to avoid dehydration from the sun and exertion.

3. Crevasse Navigation: Follow the established path to avoid hidden crevasses.

4. Pacing: Move steadily and avoid overexertion to conserve energy for higher altitudes.

Camp II to Camp III

ELEVATION:
- Camp II: 6,400 meters (21,000 feet)
- Camp III: 7,200 meters (23,625 feet)
Distance: Approximately 3 km (1.9 miles)
Terrain: Lhotse Face
Key Challenges:
- Steep and icy ascent up the Lhotse Face.
- Dealing with fixed ropes and crampons.
Guide:
1. Early Departure: Start early to avoid the risk of icefall and warming temperatures that can loosen the ice.
2. Fixed Ropes: Use fixed ropes for safety and security. Ensure your harness and ascenders are properly secured.
3. Crampons: Make sure your crampons are tightly fastened to your boots for the icy terrain.
4. Slow Ascent: Take small, deliberate steps. The steep incline and thin air make the climb physically demanding.

Camp III to Camp IV

ELEVATION:
- Camp III: 7,200 meters (23,625 feet)
- Camp IV: 7,950 meters (26,085 feet)
Distance: Approximately 2.5 km (1.5 miles)
Terrain: Yellow Band and Geneva Spur
Key Challenges:
- Crossing the Yellow Band, a section of rock strata.
- Climbing the Geneva Spur, a rocky ridge.
Guide:

1. Use of Supplemental Oxygen: Many climbers begin using supplemental oxygen at this stage to aid breathing.

2. Rock and Ice Climbing: Use fixed ropes to navigate the Yellow Band and Geneva Spur. These sections require careful footwork and handholds.

3. Conserve Energy: This segment is grueling due to the combination of altitude and technical climbing. Take frequent short breaks to rest and hydrate.

Camp IV to Summit

ELEVATION:
- Camp IV: 7,950 meters (26,085 feet)
- Summit: 8,848 meters (29,029 feet)
Distance: Approximately 1 km (0.6 miles) vertical ascent
Terrain: South Col, Balcony, South Summit, Hillary Step
Key Challenges:
- Extreme altitude (the "Death Zone") with severely limited oxygen.
- Navigating difficult sections such as the Hillary Step.
- Dealing with extreme weather conditions.
Guide:
1. Summit Push Timing: Leave Camp IV around midnight to reach the summit by early morning and descend before afternoon weather changes.

2. Use of Supplemental Oxygen: Continue using supplemental oxygen. Ensure your mask and regulator are functioning correctly.

3. The South Col: Cross the South Col and begin the climb to the Balcony (8,400 meters / 27,559 feet). Rest briefly to change oxygen bottles if needed.

4. South Summit: Continue to the South Summit (8,749 meters / 28,704 feet). This section involves steep climbing and careful navigation.

5. Hillary Step: Navigate the Hillary Step, a near-vertical rock face. Use fixed ropes and proceed cautiously.

6. Final Ascent: The final stretch from the Hillary Step to the summit is less technical but extremely exhausting. Push through with determination.

7. Reaching the Summit: Upon reaching the summit, spend a limited amount of time taking in the view and taking photos. The harsh conditions do not allow for extended stays.

Descent

SAFETY FIRST:

1. Timely Descent: Start descending immediately after summiting to avoid late afternoon weather changes.

2. Check Oxygen: Ensure you have enough supplemental oxygen for the descent.

3. Energy Management: Conserve energy and stay focused. The descent can be as challenging as the ascent.

Summary

CLIMBING MOUNT EVEREST requires meticulous planning, unwavering determination, and the ability to adapt to ever-changing conditions. Each stage from Base Camp to the summit presents unique challenges that must be approached with caution and respect for the mountain. With the right preparation and mindset, reaching the summit of Everest is a monumental achievement that few can claim.

Challenges and Hazards at Each Stage

CLIMBING MOUNT EVEREST is fraught with numerous challenges and hazards, each unique to different stages of the ascent. Understanding and preparing for these difficulties is crucial for a successful and safe climb.

#Base Camp to Camp I

- KHUMBU ICEFALL: ONE of the most dangerous sections, with moving ice blocks and deep crevasses. The Icefall is subject to avalanches and serac collapses.
    - Crevasse Crossing: Climbers must navigate crevasses using ladders, which requires balance and confidence.

#Camp I to Camp II

- WESTERN CWM: DESPITE being a relatively flat area, it acts like a solar oven, making it extremely hot during the day. Sunburn and dehydration are common issues.
    - Hidden Crevasses: The path is not always stable, and hidden crevasses pose significant risks.

#Camp II to Camp III

- LHOTSE FACE: A STEEP, icy wall that requires technical climbing skills. Falling ice and rock, as well as sudden weather changes, are major hazards.
    - Exposure: Climbers are exposed to strong winds and cold temperatures.

#Camp III to Camp IV

- YELLOW BAND AND GENEVA Spur: These sections involve mixed climbing on rock and ice, which can be technically challenging.
    - Altitude: Climbers enter the "Death Zone" (above 8,000 meters), where oxygen levels are critically low.

#Camp IV to Summit

- DEATH ZONE: SEVERE altitude sickness, extreme cold, and wind are constant threats.
    - Hillary Step: This narrow, near-vertical rock face just below the summit can be a bottleneck, leading to delays and increased exposure to harsh conditions.
    - Summit Fever: The psychological drive to reach the summit can lead to poor decision-making and increased risk-taking.

The Physiological and Psychological Effects of the Death Zone

THE "DEATH ZONE" IS the altitude above 8,000 meters (26,247 feet), where the oxygen level is insufficient to sustain human life for extended periods.

#Physiological Effects

- HYPOXIA: LOW OXYGEN levels lead to severe hypoxia, causing confusion, impaired judgment, and decreased physical performance.
    - Pulmonary and Cerebral Edema: Fluid accumulation in the lungs (HAPE) or brain (HACE) can be fatal if not treated immediately.
    - Extreme Cold: Risk of frostbite and hypothermia increases due to severe cold and wind chill.

- Muscle Deterioration: Muscle mass and strength decline rapidly due to prolonged exposure to low oxygen levels and physical exertion.

#Psychological Effects

- MENTAL FATIGUE: PROLONGED exposure to extreme conditions leads to significant mental fatigue, reducing the ability to make sound decisions.
- Isolation and Fear: The harsh environment can induce feelings of isolation, fear, and despair, which can negatively impact mental resilience.
- Hallucinations: Severe hypoxia can cause hallucinations and disorientation, further complicating the climb.

Tips for Maintaining Physical and Mental Health

MAINTAINING BOTH PHYSICAL and mental health is crucial for a successful ascent of Mount Everest. Here are some tips to help you stay in top condition:

#Physical Health

1. Acclimatization: Follow a strict acclimatization schedule to allow your body to adjust to the altitude gradually. Take rest days as needed.

2. Hydration: Drink plenty of fluids to stay hydrated. Use water purification methods to ensure safe drinking water.

3. Nutrition: Eat a balanced diet with high-calorie, nutrient-dense foods. Include carbohydrates for energy and proteins for muscle repair.

4. Supplemental Oxygen: Use supplemental oxygen above Camp III to aid in breathing and reduce the risk of hypoxia.

5. Medical Supplies: Carry essential medications, including those for altitude sickness, pain relief, and any personal prescriptions.

#Mental Health

1. Positive Attitude: Maintain a positive mindset. Focus on the journey and the experience rather than just the summit.

2. Mindfulness and Relaxation: Practice mindfulness and relaxation techniques, such as deep breathing, meditation, or visualization, to reduce stress and anxiety.

3. Support System: Rely on your climbing team for support. Share your feelings and concerns with your teammates and guide.

4. Mental Preparation: Prepare mentally for the challenges ahead. Visualize different scenarios and how you would handle them.

5. Rest and Sleep: Ensure you get adequate rest and sleep. Use earplugs and an eye mask if necessary to block out noise and light.

Conclusion

CLIMBING MOUNT EVEREST is a monumental challenge that requires careful preparation, physical fitness, mental resilience, and a deep respect for the mountain's dangers. By understanding the challenges and hazards at each stage, recognizing the physiological and psychological effects of the Death Zone, and maintaining your physical and mental health, you can increase your chances of a safe and successful ascent.

Chapter 9:
Summit Day

SUMMIT DAY ON MOUNT Everest is the culmination of months, if not years, of preparation, training, and determination. It is the most critical and challenging part of the climb, where every decision and action can make the difference between success and failure, safety and danger. This chapter covers the essential final preparations, timing, and strategy for a successful summit bid.

Final Preparations

THE NIGHT BEFORE SUMMIT day is crucial for making final preparations. Every detail must be meticulously planned to ensure a smooth ascent.

#Gear Check

- CLOTHING: ENSURE YOU are wearing multiple layers of high-quality, insulated clothing. Check that your base layers, mid-layers, and outer layers are in good condition and properly fitted.
    - Boots and Crampons: Verify that your boots are warm and comfortable. Ensure your crampons are securely attached to your boots.
    - Oxygen System: Test your supplemental oxygen system, including the mask, regulator, and oxygen bottles. Make sure everything is

functioning correctly and that you have enough oxygen for both the ascent and descent.

- Headlamp: Check your headlamp and carry spare batteries. You'll start the climb in the dark, so reliable lighting is essential.

- Safety Gear: Double-check your harness, carabiners, and any other safety gear. Ensure everything is in good working order.

- Safety Briefing: Your expedition leader will conduct a final briefing, outlining the ascent route, safety protocols, communication strategies, and turnaround times. Pay close attention and ask any questions you may have.

Mental Preparation

- REVIEW THE ROUTE: Mentally go over the route from Camp IV to the summit. Familiarize yourself with key landmarks and challenging sections.

- Set Goals: Set realistic goals for the climb. Focus on reaching intermediate points such as the Balcony and South Summit before aiming for the final push to the top.

- Visualize Success: Visualization can be a powerful tool. Picture yourself successfully reaching the summit and descending safely.

Nutrition and Hydration

- HYDRATE: DRINK PLENTY of water before going to bed to ensure you are well-hydrated. Dehydration can impair performance and increase the risk of altitude sickness.

- Eat a High-Calorie Meal: Consume a meal rich in carbohydrates and proteins. This will provide the energy needed for the grueling climb ahead.

- Snacks: Pack high-energy snacks such as energy bars, nuts, and dried fruit. Keep them easily accessible for quick energy boosts during the climb.

#Rest

- SLEEP: TRY TO GET as much rest as possible, even if it's difficult to sleep at high altitude. A few hours of sleep can make a significant difference in your energy levels and mental clarity.

Timing and Strategy

PROPER TIMING AND A well-thought-out strategy are critical for a successful summit day. The key is to start early, move efficiently, and make sound decisions based on conditions and personal health.

#Start Early

- DEPARTURE TIME: MOST teams leave Camp IV around midnight or 1 AM. Starting early maximizes your chances of reaching the summit and descending safely before afternoon weather conditions deteriorate.
    - Avoid Crowds: Starting early helps avoid traffic jams on critical sections such as the Hillary Step. Crowds can significantly slow your progress and increase exposure to the elements.

#Pacing and Energy Management

- STEADY PACE: MAINTAIN a steady, sustainable pace. Avoid the temptation to rush, as this can lead to exhaustion and mistakes.
    - Rest Stops: Take short, regular breaks to rest, hydrate, and eat. Limit breaks to avoid cooling down too much and losing momentum.

- Listen to Your Body: Pay attention to your body's signals. If you feel signs of severe fatigue, altitude sickness, or other issues, assess your condition honestly. Safety should always come first.

Key Sections

- THE BALCONY (8,400 meters / 27,560 feet): This is the first major landmark. Rest briefly, change oxygen bottles if needed, and enjoy the view of the Himalayan range.
- South Summit (8,749 meters / 28,704 feet): This false summit is a crucial checkpoint. From here, you can see the final stretch to the true summit. Take another short rest, assess your condition, and prepare for the final push.
- The Hillary Step: This 12-meter (40-foot) rock face is the last major obstacle. Use fixed ropes and take your time. Once past the Hillary Step, the summit is within reach.

Summit Push

- FINAL ASCENT: THE climb from the South Summit to the true summit is less technical but extremely exhausting. Stay focused, maintain your pace, and keep moving forward.
- Summit: Upon reaching the summit, spend only a few minutes to take photos and appreciate the achievement. Prolonged exposure at this altitude is dangerous.

Descent Strategy

- IMMEDIATE DESCENT: Begin your descent immediately after summiting. The goal is to return to Camp IV as quickly and safely as possible.

- Monitor Oxygen Levels: Ensure you have enough oxygen for the descent. Check your equipment regularly.

- Stay Alert: Fatigue and euphoria can impair judgment. Stay focused and make careful decisions, especially on technical sections like the Hillary Step and the Lhotse Face.

Conclusion

SUMMIT DAY IS THE PINNACLE of your Everest expedition. It demands careful preparation, strategic planning, and unwavering determination. By ensuring your gear is in top condition, maintaining a steady pace, and making prudent decisions, you can increase your chances of a successful and safe ascent to the top of the world. Remember, the ultimate goal is not just to reach the summit, but to return safely to tell the tale.

Dealing with Extreme Conditions

SUMMIT DAY ON MOUNT Everest presents some of the most extreme conditions on Earth. Climbers must be prepared to face harsh weather, severe cold, and the physiological challenges of high altitude.

#Harsh Weather

UNPREDICTABLE WEATHER: Weather on Everest can change rapidly. Clear skies can quickly turn into snowstorms, and high winds can create dangerous conditions.

- Weather Forecasts: Keep up-to-date with the latest weather forecasts from reliable sources. Make summit attempts only during favorable weather windows.

- Shelter: In case of sudden weather changes, seek shelter immediately. This could mean retreating to a lower camp or finding a protected area on the mountain.

High Winds: Winds on the upper slopes can exceed 100 mph, making it difficult to stand, let alone climb.

- Windproof Gear: Wear windproof clothing and ensure all skin is covered to prevent frostbite.

- Staying Low: In high winds, stay low to the ground to reduce exposure. Move cautiously to maintain balance.

Severe Cold

EXTREME COLD: TEMPERATURES on the summit can drop below -30°C (-22°F), and with wind chill, it can feel even colder.

- Layering: Wear multiple layers of clothing. Start with moisture-wicking base layers, add insulating layers, and finish with a windproof and waterproof outer layer.

- Gloves and Mittens: Use insulated gloves or mittens, and carry a spare pair. Hand warmers can also be helpful.

- Footwear: Ensure your boots are properly insulated and wear thick, moisture-wicking socks.

Physiological Challenges

HYPOXIA: THE LACK OF oxygen at extreme altitudes leads to hypoxia, which impairs physical and mental performance.

- Supplemental Oxygen: Use supplemental oxygen to help mitigate the effects of hypoxia. Check your oxygen equipment regularly to ensure it's working correctly.

- Breathing Techniques: Practice slow, deep breathing to maximize oxygen intake.

Altitude Sickness: Symptoms include headaches, nausea, dizziness, and fatigue.

- Monitor Health: Continuously monitor your physical condition and be aware of the symptoms of altitude sickness.

- Descent: If symptoms worsen, descend immediately to a lower altitude where more oxygen is available.

Safety Tips and Emergency Protocols

SAFETY IS PARAMOUNT on Everest. Understanding and following safety tips and emergency protocols can save lives.

#Safety Tips

BUDDY SYSTEM: ALWAYS climb with a partner. Look out for each other and maintain communication.

- Check-In Points: Establish regular check-in points with your partner to ensure both are okay.

Fixed Ropes: Use fixed ropes wherever available. Always double-check your harness and carabiners.

- Practice: Familiarize yourself with using fixed ropes and other climbing gear before summit day.

Energy Management: Conserve energy by moving at a steady pace. Avoid sudden bursts of speed that can lead to exhaustion.

- Rest Stops: Take short, frequent breaks to rest and hydrate. Avoid stopping for too long to prevent cooling down too much.

Stay Hydrated and Nourished: Dehydration and lack of nutrition can impair your physical and mental abilities.

- Regular Intake: Drink water regularly and eat high-energy snacks to maintain energy levels.

#Emergency Protocols

TURN-AROUND TIME: SET a strict turn-around time based on weather conditions and your physical state. If you haven't reached the summit by this time, start descending immediately, regardless of how close you are.

- Discipline: Adhere to the turn-around time without exception to ensure you have enough daylight and energy for a safe descent.

Altitude Sickness Protocols: Know the symptoms of severe altitude sickness, such as High Altitude Pulmonary Edema (HAPE) and High Altitude Cerebral Edema (HACE).

- Immediate Descent: If you or a team member shows symptoms of severe altitude sickness, descend immediately to a lower altitude.

- Medication: Carry medications like dexamethasone and nifedipine, which can help manage symptoms temporarily.

Communication: Maintain communication with your base camp and other team members.

- Radios: Use radios or satellite phones to stay in contact. Keep devices charged and accessible.

- Signal: Establish a clear signal or code for emergencies.

Emergency Supplies: Carry essential emergency supplies, including first aid kits, extra food, and water.

- Accessibility: Keep emergency supplies easily accessible in case of a sudden need.

Rescue Protocols: Know the rescue protocols and have a plan in place.

- Evacuation Plan: Understand the evacuation procedures for different scenarios, such as helicopter rescue for severe cases.

- Sherpa Assistance: Sherpas are highly skilled in high-altitude rescues. Rely on their expertise and follow their guidance in emergencies.

Conclusion

SUMMIT DAY ON MOUNT Everest is the most challenging and rewarding part of the climb. By being prepared to deal with extreme conditions and knowing the safety tips and emergency protocols, you can increase your chances of a successful and safe ascent. Remember, the ultimate goal is not just to reach the summit but to return safely. With careful planning, respect for the mountain, and adherence to safety practices, you can achieve the incredible feat of standing on top of the world.

Chapter 10:
The Descent

REACHING THE SUMMIT of Mount Everest is a monumental achievement, but the journey is far from over once you stand at the top. In fact, the descent is often considered more dangerous than the ascent. This chapter focuses on the importance of a safe descent, strategies for managing fatigue and resources, and the logistics of your return journey.

Importance of a Safe Descent

WHILE THE SUMMIT IS the ultimate goal for many climbers, it is critical to remember that reaching the top is only half the journey. The descent can be even more perilous due to the cumulative effects of fatigue, reduced oxygen levels, and potential changes in weather.

#Decreased Judgment and Physical Capability

- EXHAUSTION: AFTER the intense effort required to reach the summit, climbers are often extremely tired. This can lead to slower reaction times and impaired judgment.

- Altitude Effects: Prolonged exposure to high altitude can exacerbate symptoms of altitude sickness, making the descent more challenging.

- Adrenaline Crash: The rush of reaching the summit may quickly give way to exhaustion, making it harder to focus on the safe return.

#Weather and Environmental Conditions

- AFTERNOON WEATHER: Weather conditions often deteriorate in the afternoon, with increased risks of storms and high winds. Starting the descent early minimizes exposure to these hazards.
    - Temperature Drops: As the day progresses, temperatures can drop significantly, increasing the risk of frostbite and hypothermia.

Managing Fatigue and Resources

PROPER MANAGEMENT OF fatigue and resources is essential for a safe descent. Here are some strategies to help you stay focused and conserve energy.

#Pace and Rest

- STEADY PACE: MAINTAIN a steady, manageable pace. Avoid rushing, as it can lead to mistakes and increased risk of injury.
    - Regular Breaks: Take short, frequent breaks to rest, hydrate, and eat. This helps maintain energy levels and keeps you alert.
    - Breathing Techniques: Practice controlled breathing to maximize oxygen intake and reduce the effects of altitude.

#Hydration and Nutrition

- STAY HYDRATED: CONTINUE to drink water regularly to prevent dehydration, which can impair physical and mental performance.
    - High-Energy Foods: Eat high-energy foods such as nuts, energy bars, and dried fruit. These provide quick bursts of energy and are easy to consume on the go.

#Mental Focus

- STAY ALERT: FATIGUE can dull your senses and decision-making abilities. Stay alert and aware of your surroundings, especially on technical sections.

- Positive Mindset: Keep a positive mindset and remind yourself that the descent is an integral part of the journey. Focus on each step rather than the distance remaining.

Return Journey Logistics

PLANNING THE LOGISTICS of your return journey is crucial to ensure a safe and efficient descent to base camp and beyond.

#Camp IV to Lower Camps

- IMMEDIATE DESCENT: Begin your descent to Camp IV immediately after summiting. Aim to reach a lower camp, such as Camp II or Camp I, where you can rest and recover.

- Route Familiarity: Follow the same route you used for the ascent. Familiarity with the terrain can help reduce risks.

- Checkpoints: Set checkpoints along the way to monitor your progress and ensure you stay on schedule.

#Communication

- STAY IN CONTACT: MAINTAIN communication with your team and base camp. Use radios or satellite phones to report your progress and any issues.

- Emergency Signals: Have a clear understanding of emergency signals and protocols. Ensure your team knows how to signal for help if needed.

Health Monitoring

- MONITOR SYMPTOMS: Continuously monitor your health for symptoms of altitude sickness or other medical issues. Be prepared to descend further if symptoms worsen.

- First Aid: Carry a basic first aid kit and be ready to address common issues such as blisters, minor injuries, and altitude-related symptoms.

Logistics at Base Camp

- DEBRIEF: ONCE YOU reach base camp, debrief with your team and base camp manager. Discuss any issues encountered and ensure all team members are accounted for.

- Health Check: Undergo a thorough health check to identify any immediate medical needs. Address any issues promptly.

Travel Arrangements

- FLIGHTS AND TRANSPORT: Coordinate your travel arrangements from base camp to your home country. This may involve flights from Lukla (Nepal) or Lhasa (Tibet) to a major city, followed by international flights.

- Equipment Retrieval: Ensure all your equipment is accounted for and retrieved from higher camps if possible. This includes personal gear and any rented or borrowed equipment.

Rest and Recovery

- REST DAYS: PLAN FOR rest days at lower altitudes to aid in recovery before traveling further.

- Medical Attention: Seek medical attention for any persistent health issues, including altitude sickness symptoms or injuries.

The Final Word: Climbing Everest is an extraordinary feat of human endurance and perseverance. The knowledge you've gained throughout this book will equip you to make informed decisions and approach this challenging expedition with respect and a healthy dose of caution. Remember, reaching the summit is just part of the story. A safe return to Base Camp is the true measure of success.

Conclusion

DESCENDING MOUNT EVEREST safely is as critical as the ascent. Proper planning, resource management, and maintaining mental focus are key to ensuring a successful return to base camp. Remember, the ultimate goal is not just to reach the summit, but to return home safely. By adhering to these guidelines and staying vigilant, you can complete your Everest journey safely and successfully.

Chapter 11:
Post-Climb Considerations

SUMMITING MOUNT EVEREST is a life-changing experience that brings a mix of exhilaration, exhaustion, and a profound sense of accomplishment. However, the journey doesn't end when you leave the mountain. This chapter focuses on post-climb considerations, including health check-ups and recovery, sharing your experience, and the ethical responsibilities and opportunities to give back to the community.

Health Check-Ups and Recovery

AFTER THE PHYSICAL and mental strain of climbing Everest, it's crucial to prioritize your health and recovery.

#Medical Check-Ups

POST-CLIMB HEALTH ISSUES: Climbing Everest can take a toll on your body, and it's important to monitor for any lingering effects.

- Altitude-Related Issues: Even after descending, you may experience symptoms of altitude sickness, such as headaches, fatigue, or sleep disturbances.

- Frostbite and Hypothermia: Check for signs of frostbite and ensure any affected areas are treated promptly. Hypothermia can have lasting effects, so monitor your body's response to normal temperatures.

Comprehensive Health Evaluation: Schedule a thorough medical check-up soon after returning from the climb.

- Cardiovascular Health: The physical exertion of climbing can stress your heart. Have your cardiovascular health evaluated, especially if you experienced chest pain or shortness of breath during the climb.

- Respiratory Health: High altitudes can affect lung function. A respiratory check-up can help identify any issues that need attention.

#**Physical Recovery**

REST AND RECUPERATION: Give your body ample time to rest and recover.

- Sleep: Ensure you get plenty of sleep. High-altitude climbs can disrupt your sleep patterns, and your body needs rest to recover fully.

- Nutrition: Focus on a balanced diet rich in vitamins and minerals to aid recovery. Hydrate well to replenish fluids lost during the climb.

Gradual Return to Exercise: Ease back into physical activity gradually.

- Low-Impact Exercise: Start with low-impact exercises such as walking, swimming, or yoga to rebuild strength and flexibility.

- Strength Training: Gradually reintroduce strength training to regain muscle mass and endurance.

Sharing Your Experience

SHARING YOUR EVEREST experience can be incredibly rewarding and inspiring to others. It also provides an opportunity to reflect on your journey.

#**Personal Reflection**

DOCUMENTING YOUR JOURNEY: Take time to document your experience while the memories are still fresh.

- Journaling: Write about your climb in a journal, including your thoughts, challenges, and triumphs.

- Photography and Videography: Review and organize photos and videos taken during the climb. These visual memories can be powerful storytelling tools.

Public Speaking and Writing: Share your story through various mediums.

- Blogs and Articles: Write articles or blog posts about your experience. This can help others who are planning similar adventures.

- Public Speaking: Consider giving talks or presentations at schools, community centers, or climbing clubs. Sharing your story can inspire and educate others.

#Social Media and Online Communities

SOCIAL MEDIA PLATFORMS: Use social media to share your journey with a broader audience.

- Posts and Updates: Share regular updates, photos, and reflections on platforms like Instagram, Facebook, or Twitter.

- Engagement: Engage with followers and fellow climbers by responding to comments and questions.

Climbing Forums and Groups: Participate in online forums and groups dedicated to mountaineering.

- Advice and Tips: Offer advice and tips based on your experience. Your insights can be invaluable to aspiring climbers.

- Support and Encouragement: Provide support and encouragement to others preparing for similar climbs.

Ethical Considerations and Giving Back to the Community

CLIMBING EVEREST COMES with ethical responsibilities, including environmental stewardship and supporting the local communities that make these climbs possible.

#Environmental Responsibility

LEAVE NO TRACE: STRIVE to minimize your environmental impact on the mountain.

- Waste Management: Ensure all waste is packed out and disposed of properly. Support initiatives that promote clean climbs and waste reduction.

- Sustainable Practices: Advocate for and practice sustainable climbing methods. This includes minimizing the use of non-renewable resources and supporting eco-friendly gear manufacturers.

Climate Change Awareness: Use your platform to raise awareness about climate change and its impact on the Himalayas.

- Educational Outreach: Participate in educational programs that highlight the effects of climate change on mountain environments.

- Advocacy: Support policies and organizations that work to mitigate climate change and protect mountain ecosystems.

#Supporting Local Communities

ECONOMIC CONTRIBUTION: Recognize the role of local communities, especially the Sherpas, in your climbing success.

- Fair Wages and Treatment: Advocate for fair wages and proper treatment of Sherpas and other local support staff.

- Local Businesses: Support local businesses by choosing locally owned hotels, restaurants, and tour operators.

Community Projects: Contribute to community development projects in the region.

- Education and Health: Support initiatives that improve education and healthcare in local communities.

- Infrastructure: Contribute to projects that enhance local infrastructure, such as clean water systems, schools, and health clinics.

Climbing Everest is a privilege, not a right. By being a responsible climber, you can help preserve the magic of this iconic mountain for future generations.

Conclusion

SUCCESSFULLY SUMMITING Mount Everest is an extraordinary accomplishment that extends beyond personal achievement. Post-climb considerations are crucial for your health and well-being, and sharing your experience can inspire others. Additionally, ethical responsibilities and giving back to the community ensure that future generations can enjoy and respect this majestic mountain. By focusing on recovery, storytelling, and stewardship, you can honor your Everest journey and contribute positively to the broader mountaineering community.

Chapter 12:
Additional Resources

PREPARING FOR A CLIMB of Mount Everest is a monumental task that requires extensive research, training, and preparation. To aid you on this journey, this chapter provides a curated list of recommended reading and documentaries, useful websites and forums, and contacts for reputable expedition companies and gear suppliers.

Recommended Reading and Documentarie

#Books

1. "INTO THIN AIR" by Jon Krakauer
   - This gripping firsthand account of the 1996 Everest disaster provides valuable insights into the challenges and risks of climbing Everest.
   2. "Everest: The West Ridge" by Thomas F. Hornbein
   - A classic mountaineering book that details the first ascent of the difficult West Ridge route in 1963.
   3. "The Climb: Tragic Ambitions on Everest" by Anatoli Boukreev and G. Weston DeWalt
   - An alternative perspective on the 1996 Everest disaster, offering a different viewpoint from Krakauer's account.
   4. "No Shortcuts to the Top: Climbing the World's 14 Highest Peaks" by Ed Viesturs

- This book by renowned mountaineer Ed Viesturs provides insights into the mindset and preparation required for high-altitude climbing.

5. "Touching My Father's Soul: A Sherpa's Journey to the Top of Everest" by Jamling Tenzing Norgay

- Written by the son of Tenzing Norgay, this book explores the cultural and spiritual aspects of Everest climbs from a Sherpa's perspective.

#Documentaries

1. "EVEREST" (1998)

- A documentary film that follows an expedition to the summit of Everest, capturing both the beauty and dangers of the climb.

2. "Sherpa" (2015)

- This film provides an in-depth look at the lives of Sherpas and their crucial role in Everest expeditions, especially in the aftermath of the 2014 avalanche.

3. "The Summit" (2012)

- Although primarily about K2, this documentary offers valuable lessons on the risks and ethical considerations of high-altitude climbing.

4. "Everest: Beyond the Limit" (2006-2009)

- A TV series that documents several Everest expeditions, providing detailed insights into the preparation, challenges, and experiences of climbers.

5. "14 Peaks: Nothing Is Impossible" (2021)

- This documentary follows Nirmal Purja's mission to summit all 14 of the world's 8,000-meter peaks in seven months, showcasing the physical and mental endurance required for such feats.

Useful Websites and Forums

#Website

1.   [MOUNT   EVEREST: Facts   and
Information](https://www.nationalgeographic.com/environment/
article/mount-everest)
    - National Geographic provides comprehensive information on the
geography, history, and environmental aspects of Mount Everest.
    2.   [Alan   Arnette's   Everest](https://www.alanarnette.com/
everest/)
    - A highly informative site with detailed information on Everest
expeditions, including gear lists, route descriptions, and personal
accounts.
    3.   [The   Himalayan
Database](http://www.himalayandatabase.com/)
    - An archive of expedition records for the Nepal Himalayas,
offering valuable data on previous climbs.

#Forums

1. [SUMMITPOST](HTTPS://www.summitpost.org/)
    - A community-driven site with forums, trip reports, and climbing
route information for mountains worldwide, including Everest.
    2.   [Mountain   Project](https://www.mountainproject.com/
forum)
    - An active forum where climbers discuss routes, gear, and climbing
strategies.
    3.   [Reddit   -   r/Mountaineering](https://www.reddit.com/r/
mountaineering/)

- A subreddit dedicated to mountaineering, where users share advice, experiences, and answer questions related to high-altitude climbs.

Contacts for Expedition Companies and Gear Suppliers

#Expedition Companies

1. HIMALAYAN EXPERIENCE
   -   Website: [himalayanexperience.com](https://www.himalayanexperience.com/)
   - Description: Renowned for their expertise and strong safety record, offering guided climbs of Everest and other peaks.
   2. Adventure Consultants
   -   Website: [adventureconsultants.com](https://www.adventureconsultants.com/)
   - Description: Provides well-organized and professionally guided expeditions with a focus on safety and client care.
   3. International Mountain Guides (IMG)
   -   Website: [mountainguides.com](https://www.mountainguides.com/)
   - Description: Offers comprehensive expedition packages with experienced guides and excellent logistical support.
   4. Alpine Ascents International
   - Website: [alpineascents.com](https://www.alpineascents.com/)
   - Description: Known for their high success rates and focus on climber education and preparation.

#Gear Suppliers

1. REI

- Website: [rei.com](https://www.rei.com/)

- Description: A wide range of high-quality outdoor gear and clothing, with an emphasis on customer service and expertise.

2. The North Face

- Website: [thenorthface.com](https://www.thenorthface.com/)

- Description: Industry-leading gear and apparel designed for extreme conditions, trusted by many professional climbers.

3. Black Diamond Equipment

- Website: [blackdiamondequipment.com](https://www.blackdiamondequipment.com/)

- Description: Specializes in innovative climbing gear, including technical equipment and apparel.

4. Patagonia

- Website: [patagonia.com](https://www.patagonia.com/)

- Description: Offers durable, environmentally-friendly outdoor clothing and gear with a focus on sustainability.

5. Backcountry

- Website: [backcountry.com](https://www.backcountry.com/)

- Description: A comprehensive online retailer with a vast selection of outdoor gear and expert advice for climbers.

Remember, this is not an exhaustive list. Numerous resources exist to fuel your Everest research and planning endeavors. Approach your Everest climb with meticulous preparation, prioritize safety throughout your journey, and may your summit dreams come true!

Conclusion

THE JOURNEY TO SUMMIT Mount Everest is one of the most challenging and rewarding experiences a climber can undertake. With the right preparation, resources, and support, you can increase your chances of success and ensure a safe and memorable adventure. Use the recommended readings, documentaries, websites, forums, and contacts provided in this chapter to equip yourself with the knowledge and tools necessary for your climb. Whether you're seeking inspiration, detailed information, or practical advice, these resources will serve as valuable companions on your path to the top of the world.

Conclusion

Final Thoughts and Encouragement

CLIMBING MOUNT EVEREST is more than just a physical challenge; it's a journey that tests your endurance, determination, and spirit. Whether you're an experienced mountaineer or an aspiring climber dreaming of standing on the world's highest peak, the preparation and execution of such an expedition demand a holistic approach that encompasses physical training, mental preparation, and a deep respect for the mountain and its environment.

#Embrace the Journey

THE PATH TO THE SUMMIT is filled with both highs and lows. Every step you take, from the initial preparation to the final ascent, is part of a larger journey that will leave an indelible mark on your life. Embrace each moment, whether it's the rigorous training, the camaraderie with fellow climbers, or the quiet moments of introspection on the mountain. Remember, the journey is as significant as the destination.

#Learn and Adapt

FLEXIBILITY AND THE willingness to learn are crucial for a successful climb. Each expedition brings unique challenges and opportunities for growth. Listen to the advice of experienced climbers and guides, stay informed about the latest techniques and technologies, and be prepared to adapt to changing conditions on the mountain.

#Safety First

NEVER COMPROMISE ON safety. The risks associated with high-altitude climbing are real and can be life-threatening. Prioritize your health and well-being at every stage of the climb. Proper acclimatization, thorough health check-ups, and a disciplined approach to safety protocols can make the difference between a successful summit and a dangerous situation.

Inspirational Stories and Quotes

DRAWING INSPIRATION from those who have conquered Everest before you can provide motivation and insight. Here are a few stories and quotes from legendary climbers that encapsulate the spirit of mountaineering:

#Inspirational Stories

SIR EDMUND HILLARY and Tenzing Norgay
- First Ascent of Everest (1953): Sir Edmund Hillary of New Zealand and Tenzing Norgay, a Sherpa of Nepal, were the first climbers confirmed to have reached the summit of Everest. Their historic climb on May 29, 1953, remains a testament to human perseverance and partnership. Hillary's reflection on reaching the top—"We knocked the bastard off"—captures the sheer determination required to achieve such a feat.
Junko Tabei
- First Woman to Summit Everest (1975): Junko Tabei of Japan became the first woman to reach the summit of Everest on May 16, 1975. Her journey was marked by resilience and breaking barriers in

a male-dominated sport. Tabei's accomplishment continues to inspire women climbers around the world.

Reinhold Messner

- First Solo Ascent and Oxygen-Free Climb (1980): Reinhold Messner, an Italian mountaineer, made the first solo ascent of Everest and did so without supplemental oxygen. His approach emphasized self-reliance and the purist style of mountaineering, pushing the boundaries of what was thought possible.

#Inspirational Quotes

EDMUND HILLARY

- "It is not the mountain we conquer, but ourselves."

- This quote highlights the personal growth and inner journey that climbing Everest entails. The challenges faced on the mountain mirror the internal struggles and triumphs of the climber.

Tenzing Norgay

- "To me, it was not only a question of whether I could climb the mountain, but whether the spirit of humankind could triumph over the adversity of nature."

- Norgay's words reflect the broader significance of mountaineering as a testament to human spirit and resilience.

Reinhold Messner

- "Mountains are not fair or unfair, they are just dangerous."

- This quote serves as a sobering reminder of the inherent risks of climbing and the respect that climbers must maintain for the natural world.

Junko Tabei

- "I can't understand why men make all this fuss about Everest—it's only a mountain."

- Tabei's modesty belies the incredible challenges she overcame, underscoring her strength and determination.

Final Encouragement

EMBARKING ON AN EVEREST expedition is a monumental undertaking that demands the best of you. As you prepare for this journey, remember that you are part of a legacy of explorers who have dared to push the boundaries of human potential. Stay focused, train diligently, and approach each step with a sense of respect and wonder.

Your climb will not only be a testament to your physical and mental fortitude but also a profound journey of self-discovery. Embrace the challenges, celebrate the milestones, and never lose sight of the reasons that drew you to this extraordinary adventure. Whether you reach the summit or not, the experience will leave you with memories and lessons that will last a lifetime.

Safe travels, and may your journey to the top of the world be filled with achievement, inspiration, and unforgettable moments.

Appendices

Sample Packing List

PACKING FOR AN EXPEDITION to Mount Everest requires meticulous planning and attention to detail. Below is a comprehensive list of essential items you'll need for the climb. This list is broken down into categories to ensure you have everything required for a successful and safe ascent.

Clothing
- Base Layers:
- Moisture-wicking thermal tops and bottoms
- Lightweight long-sleeve shirts
- Thermal underwear
- Insulation Layers:
- Fleece jacket or down sweater
- Insulated pants
- Outer Layers:
- Waterproof and windproof jacket (Gore-Tex or similar)
- Waterproof and windproof pants
- Headwear:
- Warm hat or beanie
- Balaclava or neck gaiter
- Sun hat
- Handwear:
- Lightweight liner gloves
- Insulated gloves
- Waterproof gloves or mittens

- Footwear:
- Insulated mountaineering boots
- Climbing crampons compatible with your boots
- Gaiters
- Trekking shoes or boots for lower altitudes
- Wool or synthetic socks (several pairs)

Climbing Gear
- Climbing harness
- Carabiners (locking and non-locking)
- Ice axe
- Ascenders and descenders
- Ropes (fixed and dynamic)
- Helmet
- Prusik cords
- Snow stakes or pickets

Camping and Sleeping Gear
- High-altitude tent
- Sleeping bag rated for -20°F (-30°C) or lower
- Sleeping pad (foam and inflatable)
- Bivy sack (optional)

Technical Equipment
- GPS device
- Satellite phone
- Headlamp with extra batteries
- Portable solar charger or power bank
- Two-way radios (for team communication)
- Altimeter watch
- Portable oxygen system and spare canisters

Personal Items
- Trekking poles
- Sunglasses with UV protection
- Glacier glasses with side shields

- Sunscreen (high SPF) and lip balm
- First aid kit (personal medications, blister care, etc.)
- Personal hygiene items (toothbrush, toothpaste, wet wipes)
- High-energy snacks and supplements
- Water bottles and hydration system
- Pee bottle (for high camps)

Emergency Contact Numbers

HAVING ACCESS TO EMERGENCY contacts is crucial for safety and quick response in case of an incident. Below are essential contacts you should have readily available during your expedition:

Nepal
- Nepal Police: 100
- Tourist Police Kathmandu: +977 1 4247041
- Nepal Mountaineering Association (NMA): +977 1 4378855
- Embassy of Your Home Country: (Find specific contact details based on your nationality)

Tibet (China)
- Chinese Emergency Services: 110
- Tibet Mountaineering Association: +86 891 6821217
- Embassy of Your Home Country: (Find specific contact details based on your nationality)

International Contacts
- Global Rescue: +1 617 459 4200
- International SOS: +1 215 942 8226
- Local Expedition Company Emergency Contact: (Get the specific contact from your expedition provider)
- Personal Emergency Contact: (Family or friends)

Glossary of Climbing Terms

UNDERSTANDING COMMON climbing terms is essential for effective communication and safety during your expedition. Below is a glossary of key terms:

General Terms

- ACCLIMATIZATION: THE process of gradually adapting to high altitudes to prevent altitude sickness.
   - Altitude Sickness (AMS): Illness caused by the body's inability to adjust to high altitude, characterized by headaches, nausea, and fatigue.
   - Base Camp: The main encampment and logistical hub at the foot of a mountain.
   - Crampons: Metal spikes attached to boots to provide traction on ice and snow.

Climbing Equipment

- ASCENDER: A MECHANICAL device that grips the rope, allowing a climber to ascend.
   - Belay: The technique of controlling the rope to protect a climber from falling.
   - Carabiner: A metal loop with a spring-loaded gate used to connect components in climbing systems.
   - Ice Axe: A multi-purpose tool used by climbers for balance and self-arrest on ice.

Climbing Techniques

- ABSEIL (OR RAPPEL): The technique of descending a fixed rope using a friction device.

- Lead Climbing: Climbing where the lead climber places protection (gear) as they ascend.

- Sherpa: A member of the ethnic group from the Himalayas renowned for their mountaineering skills and support roles in expeditions.

- Summit: The highest point of a mountain.

Safety and Health

- CREVASSE: A DEEP CRACK in a glacier or ice sheet.

- Death Zone: The altitude above 8,000 meters (26,247 feet) where the oxygen level is insufficient to sustain human life for an extended period.

- Fixed Rope: A rope that is anchored in place along a route to provide climbers with security.

- Self-Arrest: A technique used to stop a fall by using an ice axe or other tool to dig into the snow or ice.

This appendices section provides you with critical information and tools to enhance your preparation and safety for your Everest expedition. By thoroughly understanding and utilizing these resources, you can better navigate the complexities of high-altitude climbing and ensure a more successful and rewarding experience.

Summary of All Chapters

Introduction

THE INTRODUCTION SETS the stage for the book, "How to Summit Mount Everest: A Complete Travel and Tourist Guide," by providing an overview of what readers can expect. It covers the history of Mount Everest exploration, highlighting significant milestones and the allure that drives climbers to take on this monumental challenge. This section also emphasizes the importance of thorough preparation and respect for the mountain.

Chapter 1: Understanding Mount Everest

THIS CHAPTER DELVES into the geography, weather, and key landmarks of Mount Everest. It explains the mountain's location on the border between Nepal and Tibet, the climatic conditions that climbers will face, and the significance of landmarks like Base Camp, the Khumbu Icefall, and the South Col. Understanding these elements is crucial for planning a successful expedition.

Chapter 2: Preparing for the Climb

PREPARATION IS KEY to a successful Everest expedition. This chapter covers the physical and mental preparation needed, including training routines and endurance building. It addresses health considerations such as altitude sickness and necessary immunizations and medications. The chapter also outlines the essential permits and paperwork, including climbing permits and insurance requirements.

Chapter 3: Essential Gear and Equipment

THIS CHAPTER PROVIDES a detailed guide on the gear and equipment needed for an Everest climb. It covers clothing and layering strategies to protect against extreme weather, essential climbing gear like ropes, crampons, and ice axes, and the technology and gadgets that can aid climbers, such as GPS devices, satellite phones, and oxygen systems.

Chapter 4: Choosing a Route

CLIMBERS HAVE TWO MAIN routes to choose from: the South Col route in Nepal and the North Ridge route in Tibet. This chapter compares the pros and cons of each route, helping climbers decide which path is best for their skills, experience, and preferences. It provides an overview of what to expect on each route.

Chapter 5: Selecting a Guide and Support Team

HAVING A RELIABLE GUIDE and support team is essential for safety and success. This chapter discusses the importance of hiring a guide, how to choose a reputable expedition company, and the roles of Sherpas and other support staff. It emphasizes the value of experience and local knowledge.

Chapter 6: The Journey to Base Camp

GETTING TO EVEREST Base Camp is an adventure in itself. This chapter covers travel logistics, including flights to Nepal or Tibet and the trek to Base Camp. It also discusses the acclimatization process, stressing the importance of a gradual ascent and providing a suggested acclimatization schedule to help climbers adjust to the altitude.

Chapter 7: Camp Life on Everest

LIFE AT HIGH ALTITUDES comes with unique challenges. This chapter discusses the limited facilities available at various camps and the importance of maintaining proper hygiene. It also covers strategies for managing sleep, eating, and conserving energy to stay healthy and strong throughout the climb.

Chapter 8: The Climb

THIS CHAPTER PROVIDES a step-by-step guide from Base Camp to the summit, breaking down the journey into stages: Base Camp to Camp I, Camp I to Camp II, Camp II to Camp III, Camp III to Camp IV, and Camp IV to the Summit. It discusses the challenges and hazards at each stage, the effects of the Death Zone, and tips for maintaining physical and mental health.

Chapter 9: Summit Day

SUMMIT DAY IS THE CULMINATION of all your preparation. This chapter covers the final preparations, including timing and strategy, dealing with extreme conditions, and safety tips. It also includes emergency protocols to handle unexpected situations.

Chapter 10: The Descent

DESCENDING FROM THE summit can be just as challenging as the ascent. This chapter emphasizes the importance of a safe descent, managing fatigue and resources, and the logistics of the return journey. It provides practical advice for ensuring a smooth and safe trip back to Base Camp and beyond.

Chapter 11: Post-Climb Considerations

AFTER THE CLIMB, THERE are several important considerations. This chapter discusses health check-ups and recovery, sharing your experience with others, and ethical considerations, including giving back to the local community. It highlights the importance of reflecting on the journey and its impact.

Chapter 12: Additional Resources

THE FINAL CHAPTER PROVIDES a wealth of additional resources to support climbers. It includes recommended reading and documentaries for further learning, useful websites and forums for community support, and contacts for reputable expedition companies and gear suppliers. These resources offer valuable information and connections to enhance your climbing experience.

Appendices

THE APPENDICES SECTION includes practical tools and information such as a sample packing list, emergency contact numbers, and a glossary of climbing terms. This section is designed to provide quick reference material and essential information that climbers can use throughout their preparation and expedition.

Two Words

DEAR READERS AND FELLOW Climbers,

As you stand on the precipice of embarking on your journey to the summit of Mount Everest, I am filled with admiration for your courage, determination, and passion. This book, "How to Summit Mount Everest: A Complete Travel and Tourist Guide," is more than just a manual; it is a testament to the indomitable spirit that drives us to reach for the highest peaks, both literally and metaphorically.

Mount Everest is not just a mountain. It is a symbol of human aspiration, resilience, and the relentless pursuit of dreams. The path to its summit is fraught with challenges, but it is also paved with moments of profound beauty, personal growth, and unparalleled achievement. Every step you take, every breath you draw in the thin mountain air, brings you closer not just to the top of the world, but to a deeper understanding of yourself and your capabilities.

In preparing for this climb, you have already demonstrated extraordinary commitment. You have trained your body, honed your skills, and nurtured your spirit. Remember, the journey is as important as the destination. The lessons you learn, the friendships you forge, and the obstacles you overcome will stay with you long after you have left the mountain behind.

As you navigate the complexities of this expedition, keep in mind that you are part of a legacy of explorers who have pushed the boundaries of what is possible. Draw strength from their stories, and let their triumphs inspire you. Believe in yourself, trust in your preparation, and approach each challenge with a mindset of perseverance and positivity.

Climbing Everest is not just a test of physical endurance; it is a journey that demands mental fortitude and emotional resilience. There will be moments of doubt and difficulty, but also moments of awe and elation. Embrace them all, for they are part of the transformative power of this incredible adventure.

I extend my deepest gratitude to all who have made this book possible, from the experienced climbers who have shared their insights to the dedicated support teams who ensure the safety and success of every expedition. Thank you to the Sherpas, whose knowledge, strength, and hospitality are invaluable. To the readers, thank you for trusting this guide to be part of your journey. Your dreams and ambitions inspire us all.

In closing, I leave you with this thought: The summit of Everest is a magnificent goal, but the true summit lies within you. It is the person you become in the pursuit of your dreams. May your climb be safe, your spirit be strong, and your journey be filled with unforgettable moments.

Wishing you success and safe travels,

Veena Singh Chauhan

Remember, whether you reach the top or not, you have already achieved greatness by daring to dream and strive. Every climber, every adventurer, every dreamer adds to the tapestry of human endeavor. Thank you for being part of this incredible journey.

Namaste and safe climbing.

Images & Illustrations

Note: - There are only few of images for full understanding and real view you can use You Tube, or search for more, note images may be difference from real due to AI, weather conditions, Etc.

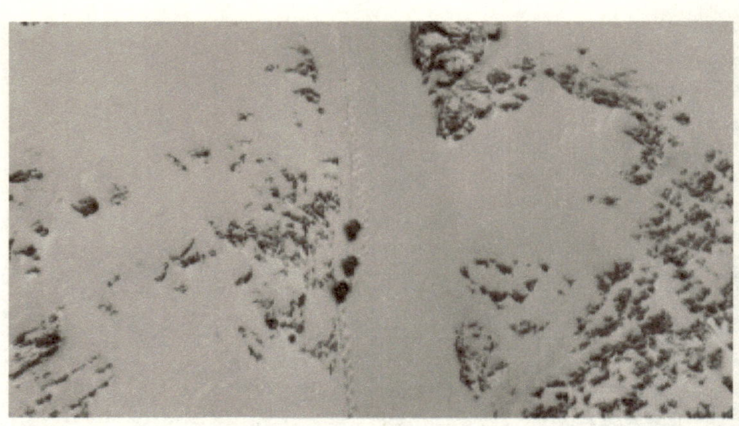

EVEREST BASE CAMP

| Page

Don't miss out!

Visit the website below and you can sign up to receive emails whenever Veena Singh Chauhan publishes a new book. There's no charge and no obligation.

https://books2read.com/r/B-A-XTICB-BUUJD

BOOKS 2 READ

Connecting independent readers to independent writers.

Also by Veena Singh Chauhan

Tourist Guide's
Know About "Taj Mahal" - The Symbol of Love - A Comprehensive
Guide
Know About "Lakshadweep" - A Tropical Paradise - A Comprehensive
Guidebook
How to Summit Mount Everest: A Complete Travel and Tourist
Guide

www.ingramcontent.com/pod-product-compliance
Lightning Source LLC
Chambersburg PA
CBHW031413150726
47989CB00002B/640